Linux Universe

3rd edition

Springer

New York
Berlin
Heidelberg
Barcelona
Budapest
Hong Kong
London
Milan
Paris
Santa Clara
Singapore
Tokyo

Stefan Strobel   Rainer Maurer   Stefan Middendorf

Linux Universe

Installation and Configuration

3rd edition

Translation by Robert Bach

 Springer

Stefan Strobel
Schlegelstraße 19
D-74074 Heilbronn
Germany

Rainer Maurer
Jakob-Haspel-Str. 18
D-74708 Heilbronn
Germany

Stefan Middendorf
Schwindstr. 7
D-74074 Heilbronn
Germany

The authors can be reached at the following e-mail address:
linux@hn-net.de

Further information about Linux Universe can be obtained at
http://www.springer-ny.com/samples/linux/linux.html

Portions of this text have been taken from Linux—Vom PC Zur Workstation, Second Edition, published by Springer-Verlag, Heidelberg.

Library of Congress Cataloging-in-Publication Data
Strobel, Stefan, 1970–
    Linux Universe : installation and configuration / Stefan Strobel,
Rainer Maurer, Stefan Middendorf.
        p.   cm.
    Includes bibliographical references and index.
    ISBN 0-387-94879-1 (softcover : alk. paper)
    1. Linux.   2. Operating systems (Computers)   I. Maurer, Rainer.
II. Middendorf, Stefan.   III. Title.
QA76.76.O63S766   1997
005.4′469—dc21   96-53012

Printed on acid-free paper.

Production managed by William Imbornoni; manufacturing supervised by Rhea Talbert.
Camera copy from the authors' TEX files.
Printed and bound by Hamilton Printing Company, Rensselaer, NY.
Printed in the United States of America.

9 8 7 6 5 4 3 2 1

ISBN 0-387-94879-1 Springer-Verlag New York Berlin Heidelberg SPIN 10552766

Contents

Acknowledgments

We wish to expressly convey our gratitude to the following persons, who actively contributed to the production of this book: Ruediger Helsch and the people from Unifix.

We also thank our translator, Bob Bach, for the synergy and the brutal night shifts that he shared with us in the final stages of preparing the manuscript for production.

These CDs could never have been produced without the preliminary work of Linus Torvalds and the international Linux network community that combined its energy to make Linux what it is today, and the pioneering efforts of Richard Stallman, founder of the Free Software Foundation, and the dedicated FSF network community that gave Linux a home in a broad base of software support.

## Chapter 1

Introduction

For some time 32-bit machines have been a hot topic in the world of PCs. It seems that more powerful operating systems will soon be displacing DOS. Meanwhile, at least in the professional literature, lively discussion has been raging about what the future standard will be. Two alternatives seem to be emerging for the domain of server operating systems: Windows NT, and UNIX variants such as   UNIX vs. Windows NT
Solaris 2, UnixWare, and NextStep 486. In this context OS/2 plays no significant role since it is seen more as a competitor to Windows in its current version and future 32-bit versions.

We cannot yet predict which system will finally predominate. However, the significant rise in the power of hardware in recent years has unleashed the demand for a modern operating system that makes use of these developments. Under a modern server operating system, the borderline between classical UNIX workstations and high-end   workstations
PCs will tend to become more fluid.

1.1   Historical perspectives on Linux

An extremely powerful alternative to the above proprietary systems has evolved far from all the big debates on strategy. The system is Linux, a UNIX system for Intel processors that is available for free.

Linux was developed by a young Finnish student named Linus Torvalds. His initial goal was not to develop a full-scale operating system, however. At first he only wanted to acquaint himself with and understand the special task-switching commands of the 80386 processor. To compile his test program, he used MINIX, a   386 processor
pedagogical operating system by Andrew Tannenbaum for teaching and learning operating systems.

1

Yet, due to its didactic orientation, MINIX had some shortcomings. The ambitious student soon exhausted the possibilities of the UNIX-like system. From his test program, he began step by step to

kernel

develop a small operating system (kernel) that ran in the protected mode of the 80386 and thus optimally exploited the processor.

After the task switcher, Torvalds wrote a simple keyboard driver to allow him to work interactively with the system. At this point Linux still relied on parts of the MINIX system, but that was soon to change.

To avoid having to develop a new file system as well, Torvalds

MINIX file system

decided to adopt the MINIX file system. This not only saved him a great deal of work, but also provided from the start a stable system for managing the hard disk. After a few months the developer considered the system to be mature enough to present it to a more general public.

In August 1991 the complete source code of Linux appeared

FTP server

for the first time on Finland's largest FTP server (Internet address `nic.funet.fi`). It was announced as a "freely distributable MINIX clone" and caught the attention of only a few interested parties on the network. Only two months later, Torvalds published the next version (0.02), which contained some rudimentary UNIX commands. The accompanying GNU compiler (gcc) permitted the compilation of small C programs and thus enabled the porting of a UNIX shell (bash).

POSIX

The early decision to adhere to POSIX, a family of standards of the Institute of Electrical and Electronics Engineers (IEEE), played a deciding role in ensuring the portability of standard UNIX software to today's Linux. However, it took until the end of the year before Linux received more widespread notice. The breakthrough came on January 5, 1992, with version 0.12. Linux had attained sufficient power to interest a larger community of developers. The system

swapping

had meanwhile acquired a swapping mechanism that gave it an unequivocal edge over MINIX.

interested developers

Over time an ever-increasing number of interested developers were sending corrections and suggestions for improvements to Finland and thus participating in the improvement of the Linux system. Early developments contributed in this way include the

POSIX Job Control in version 0.12 and the switchable virtual consoles.

The Internet proved to be an important tool for the rapid development of Linux. The Internet is a wide-area network (WAN), an information highway connecting more than six million computers and allowing the fast exchange of all kinds of information. The Internet permits Linux developers to exchange comments, improvements, and programs.

Early on, Torvalds was bombarded with over 60 e- mail messages per day, which he could hardly read and answer. Only after several discussion groups for Linux were set up did the flood of mail subside. Today there are several newsgroups concerned with Linux. The most important is `comp.os.linux.announce` (c.o.l.a.), where new developments and program versions are announced. Mailing lists were set up for Linux developers to permit a similar kind of information exchange

In addition to letters and information, files can be exchanged via the Internet, which makes it possible to organize the distributed development of larger software systems, as Linux so impressively demonstrates.

The rapid flow of information proves to be a tangible advantage not only for developers but also for users of Linux. If the user encounters any problems during installation or detects errors during operation, then with a little luck and the Internet, an adequate solution is only a couple of hours away. Even commercial service contracts seldom provide such extensive support.

Naturally, not every Linux user has access to the Internet, but even then the user is not deserted. Many mailbox networks have set up Linux discussion groups, so that a modem suffices for keeping on top of things.

An interesting aspect of Linux history is that there was never a strict hierarchy or authority that managed the development in any way. Rather, the project has been fueled by the enthusiasm of many individual Internetters who continue to contribute new improvements and suggestions. These are often professional developers or employees of large institutions who contribute their free time.

Internet

discussion groups

mailing lists

support

mailboxes

participatory
development

3

Although Linus Torvalds continues to handle the concrete further development of the kernel, quite a few competent allies have taken over other areas of the system. Such areas include the porting and maintenance of the GNU C compiler and the C libraries for Linux, the maintenance and adaptation of the X Window System, and networking. Other Linux devotees are working on user and system documentation, or assembling an installable system on diskettes or CD-ROM.

GNU C

X Window System

source code

Free source code is available not only for the kernel but also for most application programs. They come primarily from the huge UNIX freeware archives on the Internet. Periodically via the Internet a software catalog (Linux Software Map) is distributed; it currently contains some 1300 software packages. There is scarcely a domain for which some suitable software cannot be found.

software catalog

public domain

Since much development at American universities is carried out with UNIX, and such developments become public domain, many implementations in the area of research are available for Linux. One example is compilers for both well-known and more obscure programming languages. Also, the database systems Ingres and Postgres from the University of California at Berkeley have been ported to Linux.

Although the emphasis remains on freeware, commercial applications are also available, such as a Modula-2 compiler, a Smalltalk development system, an interface builder, CAD software, several database systems, and the OSF/Motif graphical user interface that has become a standard in the UNIX world.

OSF/Motif

1.2   Versions

Version 1.0

The further development of Linux is currently experiencing big leaps similar to the first implementation of the kernel. Version 1.0 was scheduled for December 1992 but was delayed—not because of a lack of stability, but because the functionality had not yet matched that of proprietary UNIX systems.

Thus the release of Version 1.0 was repeatedly delayed. In retrospect, Torvalds says that he should have declared the first stable and usable version 0.12 as version 1.0, for the zero in the version number apparently scared off many potentially interested parties from delving deeper into the system.

The final version 1.0 was released in March 1994, and developments continued with the version numbers 1.1x. This system of numbering led to a great deal of confusion among users and interested parties. Various CD producers have also contributed to the confusion by selling several Linux distributions with their own version numbers. Linux itself, however, is only a small component that easily fits on a disk several times when compiled. Asking about the Linux version on a CD is thus misleading. Instead, you should ask about the version of the kernel, the C library, the compiler, or X11.

distributions

Another popular misconception is that the higher the version number, the better or more stable the software is. This is not the case, however. For a long time, the Kernel 1.0 Patchlevel 9 (or 1.0.9 for short) was the only stable kernel; the kernels with 1.1.x numbers still contained many new and not yet completely polished functions. They were intended for developers and often changed several times in a single week.

This process ended with the release of version 1.2. Linux 1.2 contains drivers for the NCR SCSI chipset used in many PCI motherboards; it is a prerequisite for the latest versions of the DOS emulators and the iBCS2 emulation.

Linux 1.2

The situation is similar with the versions of the GNU C compiler: version 2.5.8 was by far more stable than version 2.6.0. So it is not possible to determine the quality of a Linux distribution solely by the numerical value of the version number. We recommend the Slackware or the **Linux Universe** distributions.

GNU C

The current version of Linux has all the important features of its commercial competitors, and due to its efficient design, it extracts much higher performance from a given hardware configuration. This applies to the graphical user interface as well as to the kernel.

maturity

1.3   Features

An option that may prove particularly interesting for use in commercial areas is the possibility of running programs for other

COFF, ELF   PC-based UNIX variations in COFF or ELF format under Linux. The Linux user has access to a practically unlimited supply

iBCS2   of professional applications with the iBCS2 emulator that was specifically developed for this purpose. DOS programs also run

DOS   with a DOS emulator. An emulator to directly execute MS-Windows programs under X11 is not yet entirely ready, but it does already promise some interesting perspectives for the future.

Contrary to many other UNIX systems, Linux already employs

X Window System   the newest version of the X Window System, X11R6. Additional Linux features that proprietary UNIX systems seldom provide include the support of INMOS transputer boards and the option to run TCP/IP via the serial or parallel port. Direct kernel support for ISDN boards for fast network connections over long distances makes Linux interesting for communication tasks. However, since there is no roadmap for the further development of Linux, the system will surely provide some surprises along the way.

pronunciation   Even insiders often mispronounce the word "Linux." Many users consider it an American term and pronounce it with an English long i and short u. The Finnish pronunciation is the correct one, amounting to "lee-nooks" for an English speaker.

1.4   UNIX development and standards

Ritchie & Thompson   The history of UNIX dates back well into the 1970s. In 1971 Dennis Ritchie and Ken Thompson at AT&T's Bell Laboratories developed the first version. With the availability in 1973 of the compiler

C   language C, which had evolved from BCPL and B, most of the UNIX system was rewritten, which later proved to be a great advantage for porting the system to other processors.

AT&T   Due to an agreement with the U.S. government, AT&T could not market its quite successful system. Therefore, AT&T gave UNIX as source code, although without support, to universities, where its popularity grew. With Version 7 in 1979, AT&T announced a change in its licensing policy: UNIX source code would only be provided for a fee. This prompted the University of California

BSD UNIX   at Berkeley to develop its own variant, BSD (Berkeley Software Distribution) UNIX. In 1983 AT&T announced the marketing of its

enhanced System V. The System V Interface Definition specified the   System V
programming interface to this system.

Companies like Sun Microsystems, Microsoft, and DEC
developed their own versions of UNIX (SunOS, Xenix, ULTRIX),
which in time unnecessarily encumbered the porting of software
between these systems. In order to merge the two main branches of
UNIX (BSD and System V), in 1990 AT&T propagated its Release 4   System V Release 4
of System V as a new standard that encompasses all previous variants
of UNIX.

Other institutions also have recognized the need for a   standardization
standardization of UNIX. The Institute of Electrical and Electronic
Engineers (IEEE) developed the POSIX standard for UNIX-related   POSIX
operating systems. This standard is divided into several parts. POSIX
1003.1 describes only the lowest-level system interface; 1003.2
will define a standard for shells and commands; 1003.7 covers the
possibilities of system administration. Although POSIX is actually
based on the UNIX system interface, this standard will also be
supported by other operating systems (e.g., Windows NT).

A body consisting primarily of UNIX manufacturers has
released another standard. Although the X/Open Portability Guide   X/Open
is based on POSIX 1003.1, it provides extensions in certain points.
Within the realm of the COSE Initiative (Common Open Software
Environment), the importance of the X/Open Consortium rose
significantly. The present goal is to release a uniform desktop-
user interface, the Common Desktop Environments (CDE) and   CDE
programmer interface for all available UNIX variants. This should
drastically reduce the effort required for porting software. Linux
adheres to the POSIX standard.

1.5   The Free Software Foundation

In addition to its orientation to the POSIX standard, Linux is also
largely subject to the General Public License (GPL) of the Free   General Public License
Software Foundation (FSF). FSF was founded about a decade ago
by Richard Stallman, the developer of the legendary GNU Emacs   Richard Stallman
editor. The organization "aims to make high-quality free software   free software

7

available to everyone." Note that *free* in the title of the organization refers to "freedom," not "zero dollars."

This kind of freedom means that copying and distributing software, including the source codes, is not to be restricted. This makes free software fundamentally different from public domain software or shareware. It is protected by copyright, and the license requirements are regulated by the GPL.

commercial distribution

Software that is subject to the GPL may also be commercially distributed, but it must be possible for anyone to copy it and pass it on. The source code must be included. If developers use free software as the basis for their own developments, then this development must also be made available under the GPL. This does not apply to software that was compiled with the GNU C compiler or edited with the GNU Emacs editor, but rather to programs using a source code that is subject to the GPL.

quality

A frequent result of this practice is an increase in the quality of software, from which everyone benefits. For instance, the Next

Objective-C

Company used the GNU C compiler as the basis of its Objective C compiler. So what was available to them was a relatively mature and freely accessible compiler. Under the GPL, the new additions were made available to the general public, so now the GNU C compiler works not only with ANSI C and C++, but also with Objective C.

GNU

The GNU project represents FSF's attempt to develop a complete operating system that can be freely copied and is largely compatible with UNIX. GNU, by the way, stands for "Gnu's not UNIX." In addition to the GNU C compiler and the Emacs editor, numerous UNIX-compatible commands and tools were developed in the course of this project that are currently used in almost all Linux distributions. What the FSF and GNU project have been lacking is an operating

Hurd

systems core. Although the GNU kernel (Hurd) was already in the works before Linux emerged, it cannot be employed yet by users. Hurd is based on the Mach-3 microkernel, and someday it may well be technologically superior to Linux.

Since quite a few UNIX commands and utilities originated in the GNU project or are at least subject to the GPL, Linux has profited from the project. At the same time, Linux fulfills the aim of the GNU

Linux & FSF

project, as the Linux kernel, together with the FSF tools and other freely accessible utilities, represents a complete UNIX system that is free of charge.

Currently, the further development of such essential elements as the C compiler and the C library is done in collaboration and is coordinated by GNU and Linux developers. Popular FTP servers now offer the interested programmer an overwhelming multitude of software that is subject to the GPL. In addition to programming languages such as C, C++, Smalltalk, Lisp, and Fortran, there are also various editors, debuggers (gdb), and even a PostScript interpreter (Ghostscript).

further developments

FTP server

## Chapter 2

Features

L inux is a free UNIX-like operating system kernel. Our **Linux Universe** distribution includes this kernel together with many tools from the Free Software Foundation's GNU project and other freely available programs and utilities. They were developed by many volunteers all over the world. Together they build a complete UNIX-like system.

To give you a better orientation, we offer the following summary of the most important features of Linux and our distribution:

- **A full-fledged, 32-bit multi-user/multitasking UNIX system**. Linux permits multiple users to execute (different) programs simultaneously and thereby fully exploits the capacity of the Intel 80386 processor and its successors. The resulting performance is definitely comparable to a classical RISC workstation.

  multi-user
  multitasking

  performance

- **Orientation to common UNIX standards** (POSIX). This provides an ideal environment for developing portable software. Available software that adheres to existing UNIX standards usually can be ported to Linux without problems.

  standards

- **Network support** (TCP/IP and others). A machine running **Linux Universe** can easily be integrated into a TCP/IP network, LanManger, Windows for Workgroups or Novell network. Linux supports common Ethernet adapters and TCP/IP connection via modem (SLIP, PPP).

  network

- **Graphical user interface** (X Window System). The **Linux Universe** system includes the current version (Release 6) of

  X Window System

OSF/Motif   the X Window System. OSF/Motif, the standard user interface for proprietary UNIX systems, can be purchased as an add-on product.

GNU

- **GNU utilities and programs**. Many of **Linux Universe**'s commands and utilities emanate from the GNU project and contribute much functional enhancement.

compatibility

- **Complete UNIX development environment**. **Linux Universe** permits the development of programs that run problem-free on other UNIX systems. In addition to the GNU C/C++/ Objective C compiler, numerous editors, and several version control systems, there are many other software development tools.

- **Runs directly from the CD-ROM**. The **Linux Universe** system is preconfigured and runs directly from the CD-ROM. It needs only minimal space on your hard drive.

- **Smart CD-ROM cache**. The **Linux Universe** distribution profits from its smart CD-ROM cache to speed up access to the files on the CD-ROM. Accessed files are automatically copied to the hard drive. The cache can be configured to allow maximum size of cached files.

- **Graphical administration tool**. The graphical tool `xadmin` supports configuration and administration of the system.

- **Complete ELF**. The entire **Linux Universe** distribution uses the new ELF link format, making it one of the first and most up to date distributions with ELF.

- **Compatibility to the IBCS2 Standard**. This allows the execution of programs in COFF and ELF format that were developed for SCO UNIX or other PC UNIX variants.

## Chapter 3

New features in Linux 2.0

- All drivers are now available as loadable modules. This allows you to keep the kernel quite lean.
- The new `kerneld` daemon loads modules dynamically as needed at run-time.
- Comfortable menu-driven kernel configuration is available in text mode and under X11.
- Windows 95 VFAT file system is supported.
- SMB protocol support permits accessing directories on Windows for Workgroups or Windows NT computers.
- IPX support enables access to Novell networks and lets you use a Linux machine as an IPX router.
- New features enable using a Linux machine as a bridge or firewall.
- Java applets and applications can be executed directly.
- One common source text tree is available for all supported platforms.
- Support for ISDN boards has been added.
- Numerous new hardware drivers have been added.

•   Linux has a new logo:

by L. Ewing

## Chapter 4

Hardware

4.1 Required hardware

Processor

Linux Universe is a 32-bit operating system for Intel processors. It requires an Intel 80386SX or higher (80386, 80486 or Pentium), because for multitasking support the operating system employs special machine commands that are available only with these processors. If your system lacks a coprocessor, you can run an emulation.

80386SX or higher

coprocessor emulation

Memory

For practical work with Linux you need at least 8 MB of RAM. Although it is possible to run the `X-Window` graphical user interface with 8 MB, 16 MB delivers a noticeable increase in speed. You can also install a swap file that Linux can then use for storing regions of memory (swapping). This certainly enhances the possibilities if you happen to have less than 16 MB.

8-16 MB

Hard disk capacity

The basic installation requires only 30 MB of hard disk storage. You need not store application programs on the hard disk because the file cache in **Linux Universe** initially retrieves application programs from the CD. If there is room on the hard disk, the file cache automatically copies the programs onto the hard disk when they are first launched. Later invocations then launch the program directly from the hard disk. We advise having at least 100 to 200 MB.

at least 30 MB

100 MB makes sense

Floppy disk drive

If the system is to be installed with a boot diskette or via NFS, you need a 3.5"/1.44 MB floppy disk drive.

Bus

Linux Universe supports all common bus systems, including ISA (AT-Bus), VLB (Local-Bus), EISA (Enhanced-ISA), and PCI.

Video adapter

Linux runs in text mode with all video adapters and under X-Windows in graphic mode with monochrome, EGA, and VGA video adapters; in fact, for many chip sets there are optimized servers (see the list starting on page 18).

Monitor

In general, all common models are supported under X-Windows. If there are problems with the built-in drivers, monitor controls can be configured as needed and adapted to your individual model. In terms of size, you really should have a 17-inch monitor, but naturally this is not a prerequisite since X-Windows can drive higher resolutions virtually (here the screen extends beyond the edge of the monitor and can be shifted with corresponding mouse actions).

17" recommended

Mouse and trackball

While a mouse is not necessary in text mode, one is required under X-Windows. **Linux Universe** supports serial mice, bus mice and PS/2 mice, with either two or three buttons. This also applies for trackballs.

Printers

Linux Universe supports all common printers (including Post-Script). You can print PostScript documents even on non-PostScript printers due to a built-in filter that handles conversion as needed.

4.2   Supported hardware

Below is a list of hardware components that are generally supported
by Linux. *Note that not all of the following devices are supported* ◄┘
by **Linux Universe**. Drivers for rare components might have to be
retrieved via FTP and then integrated via a recompilation of the
kernel.

SCSI host adapters
*   AMD AM53C974, AM79C974 (PCI) (Compaq, HP, Zeos
    onboard SCSI)
*   AMI Fast Disk VLB/EISA (BusLogic-compatible)
*   Adaptec AVA-1505/1515 (ISA) (Adaptec 152x compatible)
*   Adaptec AHA-1510/152x (ISA) (AIC 6260/6360)
*   Adaptec AHA-154x (ISA) (all models)
*   Adaptec AHA-174x (EISA) (in enhanced mode)
*   Adaptec AHA-274x (EISA)/284x (VLB) (AIC 7770)
*   Adaptec AHA-2940/3940 (PCI) (AIC 7870)
*   Always IN2000
*   BusLogic (ISA/EISA/VLB/PCI) (all models)
*   DPT PM2001, PM2012A (EATA PIO)
*   DPT Smartcache (EATA-DMA) (ISA/EISA/PCI) (all models)
*   DTC 329x (EISA) (Adaptec 154x compatible)
*   Future Domain TMC-16x0, TMC-3260 (PCI)
*   Future Domain TMC-8xx, TMC-950
*   NCR 5380
*   NCR 53c400 (Trantor T130B)
*   NCR 53c406a (Acculogic ISApport/Media Vision Premium
    3D SCSI)
*   NCR 53c7x0, 53c8x0 (PCI)
*   Pro Audio Spectrum 16 SCSI (ISA)
*   Qlogic/Control Concepts SCSI/IDE (FAS408)
    (ISA/VLB/PCMCIA)
*   Seagate ST-01/ST-02 (ISA)
*   SoundBlaster 16 SCSI-2 (Adaptec 152x compatible) (ISA)
*   Trantor T128/T128F/T228 (ISA)
*   UltraStor 14F (ISA), 24F (EISA), 34F (VLB)

17

• Western Digital WD7000 SCSI

Hard disk controllers

• 8-bit XT
• standard IDE, MFM, RLL
• enhanced IDE (EIDE)
• ESDI in ST 506 emulation
• SCSI controller: see above

CD-ROM drives

• all SCSI CD-ROM drives
• EIDE (ATAPI) CD-ROM drives
• Aztech CDA268, Orchid CDS-3110, Okano/Wearnes CDD-110, Conrad TXC
• GoldStar R420
• LMS Philips CM 206
• Matsushita/Panasonic, Creative Labs, Longshine, Kotobuki on a SoundBlaster sound card (and compatible) or on NoSound adapter
• Mitsumi
• Optics Storage Dolphin 8000AT
• Sanyo H94A
• Sony CDU31A/CDU33A
• Sony CDU-535/CDU-531
• Teac CD-55A SuperQuad

Streamers

• SCSI streamer
• QIC-02
• QIC-117, QIC-40/80 floppy streamer
• QIC-3010/3020 floppy streamer
• ATAPI streamer

Video cards

• VGA
• EGA
• ARK Logic ARK1000PV/VL, ARK2000PV

- ATI VGA Wonder series
- ATI Mach8
- ATI Mach32 (16 bpp; does not run with all Mach32 adapters)
- ATI Mach64 (16/32 bpp; support depends on RAMDAC)
- Advance Logic AL2101/2228/2301/2302/2308/2401
- Chips & Technologies 65520/65530/65540/65545
- Cirrus 542x, 543x
- Cirrus Logic 5420, 542x/5430 (16 bpp), 5434 (16/32 bpp), 62x5
- Cirrus Logic 6420/6440
- Compaq AVGA
- Diamond Viper VLB/PCI
- Genoa GVGA
- IBM 8514/A
- IBM XGA, XGA-II
- IIT AGX-010/014/015/016 (16 bpp)
- Orchid P9000
- MCGA (320x200)
- MX MX68000/MX68010
- NCR 77C22, 77C22E, 77C22E+
- Oak OTI-067, OTI-077
- OAK OTI-037/67/77/87
- RealTek RTG3106
- S3 911, 924, 801, 805, 928, 864, 964, Trio32, Trio64, 868, 968 (e.g., Miro, Spea)
- Trident TVGA8800, TVGA8900, TVGA9xxx (no support for TGUI chip sets)
- Tseng ET3000/ET4000/W32/W32i/W32p
- VGA (standard VGA, 4 bit, slow)
- Video 7/Headland Technologies HT216-32
- Weitek P9000 (16/32 bpp)
- Western Digital/Paradise PVGA1, WD90C00/10/11/24/30/31/33
- Hercules mono
- Hyundai HGC-1280
- Sigma LaserView PLUS
- VGA mono

Sound cards

* 6850 UART MIDI
* Adlib (OPL2)
* Audio Excell DSP16
* Aztech Sound Galaxy NX Pro
* ECHO-PSS cards (Orchid SoundWave32, Cardinal DSP16)
* Ensoniq SoundScape
* Gravis Ultrasound
* Gravis Ultrasound 16-bit sampling derivative
* Gravis Ultrasound MAX
* Logitech SoundMan Games (SBPro, 44kHz Stereo support)
* Logitech SoundMan Wave (Jazz16/OPL4)
* Logitech SoundMan 16 (PAS-16 compatible)
* MPU-401 MIDI
* MediaTriX AudioTriX Pro
* Media Vision Premium 3D (Jazz16)
* Media Vision Pro Sonic 16 (Jazz)
* Media Vision Pro Audio Spectrum 16
* Microsoft Sound System (AD1848)
* OAK OTI-601D cards (Mozart)
* OPTi 82C928/82C929 cards (MAD16/MAD16 Pro)
* SoundBlaster
* SoundBlaster Pro
* SoundBlaster 16 (no support for ASP chips)
* Turtle Beach Wavefront cards (Maui, Tropez)
* Wave Blaster (and derivatives)

Network adapters

* 3Com 3C501
* 3Com 3C503, 3C505, 3C507, 3C509/3C509B (ISA)/3C579 (EISA)
* AMD LANCE (79C960)/PCnet-ISA/PCI (AT1500, HP J2405A, NE1500/NE2100)
* AT&T GIS WaveLAN
* Allied Telesis AT1700
* Ansel Communications AC3200 EISA
* Apricot Xen-II

- Cabletron E21xx
- DEC DE425 (EISA)/DE434/DE435 (PCI)
- DEC DEPCA and EtherWORKS
- HP PCLAN (27245 and 27xxx models)
- HP PCLAN PLUS (27247B and 27252A)
- HP 10/100VG PCLAN (ISA/EISA/PCI)
- Intel EtherExpress
- Intel EtherExpress Pro
- NE2000/NE1000 and compatible
- New Media Ethernet
- Racal-Interlan NI5210 (i82586 Ethernet chip)
- Racal-Interlan NI6510 (am7990 lance chip), only with less than 16 MB RAM
- PureData PDUC8028, PDI8023
- SEEQ 8005
- SMC Ultra
- Schneider & Koch G16
- Western Digital WD80x3
- Zenith Z-Note/IBM ThinkPad 300 built-in adapter
- AT-Lan-Tec/RealTek parallel port adapter
- D-Link DE600/DE620 parallel port adapter
- all ARCnet adapters

ISDN adapters
- ICN ISDN
- PCBIT ISDN
- Teles ISDN

PCMCIA adapters
- 3Com 3C589, 3c589B
- Accton EN2212 EtherCard
- CNet CN30BC Ethernet
- D-Link DE650
- EFA InfoExpress SPT EFA 205 10baseT
- EP-210 Ethernet
- Farallon Etherwave
- GVC NIC-2000P Ethernet Combo

- HYPERTEC HyperEnet
- IBM Credit Card Adapter
- IC-Card Ethernet
- Katron PE-520 Ethernet
- Kingston KNE-PCM/M
- LANEED Ethernet
- Linksys EthernetCard
- Maxtech PCN2000 Ethernet
- Network General Sniffer
- Novell/National NE4100 InfoMover
- Proteon Ethernet
- PreMax PE-200 Ethernet
- RPTI EP400 Ethernet
- Socket Communications Socket EA LAN Adapter
- Thomas-Conrad Ethernet
- Volktek Ethernet
- and others

## Chapter 5

Basic installation

5.1 Overview

Before you get started, let us first give you an overview of various installation possibilities for **Linux Universe**. You can install **Linux Universe** on your hard disk in the following ways:

- **Linux Universe** can be installed on a dedicated hard-disk partition. If you do not have room for a new partition, but your DOS partition still has sufficient free space, you can use the DOS program FIPS.EXE, which is located in the main directory of the **Linux Universe** installation CD, to split your DOS partition; Linux can then be installed on this newly created partition. If you want to split a DOS partition, you must execute FIPS.EXE before you begin the actual installation. Otherwise you can carry out partitioning or repartitioning from the installation program.

  Linux partition

- If you do not have enough space for a new partition, you can install **Linux Universe** in the directory \LINUX of your DOS partition, but you must be aware that this has its price in terms of speed of execution. Furthermore, a Linux file system is superior for security reasons. On the other hand, installation on a DOS partition is ideal if you just want to try out the system and experiment with it.

  DOS partition

In any case, you will need at least 30 MB of disk space. **Linux Universe** also makes it possible to install via NFS. With the NFS installation, **Linux Universe** can be installed on a computer (client) that has a network adapter or a parallel port, but lacks a CD-ROM drive. The client can access software via the network, whereas the CD needs to be in a server machine.

Independent of the above, you can choose between two types of software installation:

- Fix installation: In the installation program you determine the packages to be installed. The installation program then copies the basic system and the selected packages onto the hard disk. After completed installation the CD can be removed from the drive. The advantage of this approach is that after installation the system is independent of the CD. The drawback is that you have available only the software contained in the selected packages. If you need other programs later, you must install the packages, although this is not a problem.

  For novices we recommend using the file cache as described below, since they might have difficulty in already selecting packages that they will need later.

- With the file cache, the software remains on the CD until it is invoked for the first time; then the file cache copies it onto the hard disk. On the next invocation the program is started directly from the hard disk. The advantage of this approach is that you only fill the hard disk with software that you actually use. After some time you could say that the system has effectively installed itself. The drawback is that the CD must remain in the drive during this installation period. Only when you are sure that everything is installed that you need can you remove the CD from the drive.

  However, when using the file cache it is still possible to install files, directories, or whole packages manually. If you know in advance that you will use certain programs intensively, you can select the corresponding packages in the installation program. These packages are then preinstalled, so that the programs contained therein no longer depend on the CD.

After **Linux Universe** has been installed, you have the following variants to boot the system:

boot variants

- After booting, Linux can be started from DOS. This can be done by hand with a batch file. However, you can define a menu

in your CONFIG.SYS that allows you to select the operating
system to boot.

- You can configure the system so that booting first goes to
the **Linux Universe** boot manager. There you can select the
partition (or the floppy disk drive) and the operating system
(Linux, DOS, OS/2) for booting.
- Especially if you want to install Linux on the second physical
hard disk, you need to install the master boot record (MBR) of
Linux Universe. This gives you a small menu on startup that
allows selection of the physical hard disk and partition (or a
floppy disk drive) for booting. Choosing the Linux partition
takes you to the **Linux Universe** boot manager.
- Linux can also be started from another boot manager such as
that of OS/2.

Note that the method used for booting Linux is completely
independent of how you installed Linux on your hard disk. When the
operating system boots, it does not care from where it was loaded.

Also read the section on partitioning (page 33) before you begin
your installation.

5.2   Booting for installation

Installation can take place in one of three ways:

- from DOS
- with a boot diskette
- from the CD-ROM drive of another computer via the Network
File System (NFS)

Installation from DOS

First terminate any installed hard disk accelerator programs (e.g.,
for SMARTDRV.EXE with smartdrv /c). Then change to the
root directory of the CD and invoke the program INSTALL.EXE.
INSTALL requires at least one parameter for the type of your CD-
ROM drive. If you invoke INSTALL without any parameters, it
displays a list of available drive types. Specify:

    sr0 for the first SCSI CD-ROM

hard disk accelerator

INSTALL.EXE

25

sr1 for the second SCSI CD-ROM

hda for an EIDE/ATAPI CD-ROM (master on first controller)

hdb for an EIDE/ATAPI CD-ROM (slave on first controller)

hdc for an EIDE/ATAPI CD-ROM (master on second controller)

hdd for an EIDE/ATAPI CD-ROM (slave on second controller)

mcd for a non-EIDE/ATAPI CD-ROM by Mitsumi

sbpcd for a Kotobuki/Matsushita/Panasonic CD-ROM model CR-521/522/523/562/563

cdu535 for a Sony CDU-535 CD-ROM

cm206cd for a Laser-Magnetic Storage drive by Philips, model CM-206

aztcd for Aztech CDA-268-01A, Orchid CD-3110, Okano CDD110, Wearnes CDD110

sonycd for Sony CDU-31A or CDU-33A

optcd for an Optics Storage 8000 AT CD-ROM

gscd for a GoldStar R420 CD-ROM

sjcd for a Sanyo CDR-H94A CD-ROM

➡ **Note:** If only one device is connected to an IDE/EIDE controller, it must be configured as master and accessed as hda or hdc.

INSTALL might terminate with a message about too little memory. In this case read the instructions in the following section. In addition, Linux might require additional information about your hardware configuration for successful booting. Here you can pass additional parameters to INSTALL after the type of the CD drive. Especially if you have a non-EIDE/ATAPI/SCSI CD-ROM or a SCSI adapter, you should use the boot option cdrom= or scsi=. The

boot options
available boot options are listed starting on page 53. After successful booting, the menu of the **Linux Universe** installation program is displayed and actual installation can begin.

Instructions for DOS memory configuration Because the pro-

lower memory area
grams INSTALL.EXE and LOADLIN.EXE are greedy for memory in the lower memory area, you might need to modify your DOS memory configuration in order to execute these programs. This

26 AUTOEXEC.BAT
might require some experimentation. Create a backup copy of your

AUTOEXEC.BAT and CONFIG.SYS files so that you can restore the   CONFIG.SYS
original version if something goes wrong. The following are some
clues for the modification of AUTOEXEC.BAT and CONFIG.SYS:

- Observe the instructions in the file LOADLIN.TXT in the root
  directory of the **Linux Universe** installation CD.
- Remove all memory-resident programs and all device drivers
  that are not absolutely necessary, such as the mouse driver and
  SMARTDRV.EXE. Actually, all you really need is the driver
  for the CD-ROM drive. You might want to retain such drivers
  as HIMEM.SYS and EMM386.SYS.
- Use the DEVICEHIGH or LOADHIGH statements to load as
  many drivers as possible into the high memory area.
- If your system has SCSI components, use the smallest driver
  for the host adapter (e.g., MINICAM.SYS).
- In CONFIG.SYS, load DOS with DOS=HIGH into the high
  memory area.

Installation with a boot diskette

Create a boot diskette as described below and then restart the
computer with it. In your BIOS setup, you might first have to enable   BIOS setup
booting from a floppy disk. We highly recommend using a name-
brand diskette for the boot diskette if possible, for the boot diskette
does not contain a table in which defective sectors are recorded. On
booting, the sectors are read sequentially from the diskette. If the
system encounters a defective sector, it crashes.

Creating a boot diskette from DOS   Change to the root directory of
the installation CD. There you will find the program RAWRITE.EXE,   RAWRITE.EXE
which copies a boot diskette image from the CD onto a diskette. The
diskette must already be low-level formatted. *Ensure that the diskette*
contains no important data, since the writing process amounts to
formatting and so irretrievably destroys any data! On invocation,
RAWRITE prompts for the name of the source file for the boot
diskette. Enter fd1440.

Then you must enter the DOS drive letter of the floppy disk
drive in which the boot diskette is to be created. RAWRITE ignores

27

any drive reassignments that you might have set with the `ASSIGN` command.

After completion of `RAWRITE` the boot diskette is ready.

Creating a boot diskette from Linux   Insert the **Linux Universe**
CD in your drive. Then mount the CD-ROM drive in the directory
/dist (if this has not already occurred) with the command

mount CD-ROM

```
mount -t iso9660 -o ro /dev/sr0 /dist
```

This example is for a SCSI CD-ROM; you should use the driver
corresponding to your system (see the list starting at the bottom of
page 25). Then create the boot diskette with the command

```
cat /dist/fd1440 > /dev/fd0
```

for the first floppy disk drive. If you use the second floppy disk drive,
specify /dev/fd1 instead of /dev/fd0.

Booting   Booting first brings you to the **Linux Universe** boot
boot manager
manager. There you select the option **Floppy**.

You might have to provide Linux with additional information on
your hardware configuration to boot successfully. Especially if you
have a non-EIDE/ATAPI/SCSI CD-ROM or a SCSI adapter, you
boot options
should use the boot option cdrom= or scsi=. These boot options
must be specified in the boot manager. A list of possible boot options
starts on page 54; a detailed description of the boot managers starts
on page 76. After successful booting, Linux displays the following
message:

```
          Welcome to the Linux Universe Install Menu guided installation!

For Help type "?".
Where is the Linux Universe runtime CD-ROM? Default devices:  1) hda   2) hdb   3
) hdc  4) hdd  5) sr0  6) sr1  7) nfs  8) mcd  9) sbpcd  10) lmscd  11) sonycd
   12) cdu535  13) aztcd  14) sjcd  15) cm206cd  16) hitcd  17) gscd  18) optcd
   19) plip0  20) plip1  21) plip2  22) bootp
Device name of CD-ROM or <Enter> for automatic search: █
```

Figure 5.1.   Selection of CD drive

Please enter the type of your CD-ROM drive:

1 for an EIDE/ATAPI CD-ROM installed as master on the first
controller

2 for an EIDE/ATAPI CD-ROM installed as slave on the first
controller

3 for an EIDE/ATAPI CD-ROM installed as master on the second
controller

4 for an EIDE/ATAPI CD-ROM installed as slave on the second
controller

5 for the first SCSI CD-ROM

6 for the second SCSI CD-ROM

8 for a non-EIDE/ATAPI CD-ROM by Mitsumi

9 for a Kotobuki/Matsushita/Panasonic CD-ROM, model
CR-521/522/523/562/563 on sound card

11 for a Sony CDU-31A/33-A CD-ROM

12 for a Sony CDU-535/531 CD-ROM

13 for Aztech CDA-268-01A, Orchid CD-3110, Okano CDD110,
Wearnes CDD110

14 for a Sanyo CDR-H94A CD-ROM (non-EIDE/ATAPI)

15 for a Laser-Magnetic Storage drive by Philips, model CM-206

17 for a GoldStar R420 CD-ROM

18 for an Optics Storage 8000 AT CD-ROM

Note: If only one device is connected to an IDE/EIDE controller, ←
it must be configured as master and you must enter 1 or 3.

Option 8 and options 19 to 22 are for network installation,
described in the next section. Next the **Linux Universe** installation
program is launched. If the CD-ROM drive is not recognized, it must
be specified more precisely with the boot option of the corresponding
driver.

NFS installation

The NFS installation allows you to install **Linux Universe** on a
computer (the client) that has no CD-ROM drive. The software
is accessed via the network, with the CD inserted in another
computer (the server). For NFS installation, we assume familiarity
with the terms *IP address* and *network mask*. You can refer

29

to explanations in the *Linux Network Administrator's Guide*
(/usr/doc/net-adm-guide-1.0.dvi.gz).

For NFS installation, you can use either of two methods:

- NFS installation can take place on an Ethernet-based network.
  The client can be configured by manually entering the addresses
  of server and client at the start of the installation; alternatively,
  you can configure the client automatically by using BOOTP
  (boot protocol). However, this requires that the server know the
  Ethernet address of the client so that the server can assign an IP
  address.
- **Linux Universe** can also be installed with a PLIP (parallel line
  IP) connection. PLIP is certainly the simplest and cheapest
  way to network two computers. The parallel ports of the two
  computers are connected with a null printer, or Laplink, cable.
  You can make such a cable yourself; see Appendix A of the
  Linux Network Administrator's Guide.

Preparing the server The prerequisite for installation via NFS
is that the corresponding driver for PLIP or the respective Ethernet
board be either compiled into the kernel or, as in the **Linux Universe**
standard kernel, available as a module.

Before beginning the installation, you must configure the
network interface of the server, if this has not already been done. For
the PLIP installation the `pointopoint` option must be specified
in the `route` command. For installation via the first parallel port,
execute the following commands:

```
ifconfig plip1 <server-IP> netmask <netmask> pointopoint <client-IP>
route add <client-IP>
```

In the `route` command you can specify the parallel port
explicitly, but normally this is not done:

```
route add <client-IP> dev plip1
```

Additionally, on the server you need to create the directory
/dist, where the installation CD is mounted; then mount the CD-
ROM drive in this directory. The following example applies for the
first SCSI drive:

```
mount -t iso9660 -o ro /dev/sr0 /dist
```

Next you must enter the directory /dist in the file /etc/
exports. This releases /dist for use via NFS. Append the
following line to the file /etc/exports:

```
/dist 193.168.1.2(ro,no_root_squash)
```

Here 193.168.1.2 represents the address of the computer
on which **Linux Universe** is to be installed. Alternatively, you
can simply uncomment the already existing line for /dist in
/etc/exports, which then makes the directory exportable to the
world.

Next the daemons mountd and nfsd must be restarted so that
the modifications in /etc/exports take effect. Do this with the
following command:

```
killall mountd nfsd; mountd; nfsd
```

If the computer has not been an NFS server before, you can omit the
killall command. Then the following suffices:

```
mountd; nfsd
```

Additional preparations for BOOTP For installation with
BOOTP, you need not specify any address, since the server assigns the
IP address to the clients. Here the client sends its Ethernet address to
the BOOTP server bootpd. The server assigns the transmitted Ethernet address an IP address on the basis of the file /etc/bootptab.
Thus, in contrast to NFS installation, BOOTP installation requires
that the server know the client's Ethernet address. Then the server
sends the assigned IP address back to the client.

First, the inetd must be configured so that queries to the
BOOTP server are forwarded; thus the file /etc/inetd.conf
must contain the line

```
bootps dgram udp wait root /usr/sbin/bootpd bootpd
```

and the file /etc/services must contain the lines

31

```
bootps 67/udp bootp
bootps 67/tcp
```

Next, in the file /etc/bootptab the client's hardware address
must be assigned an Ethernet address. In its simplest form, an entry
for the client hermes can look like this:

```
hermes:ht=ethernet:ha=0000C012FA6D:ip=192.168.1.2:sm=255.255.255.0
```

More detailed information can be found in the man pages for
bootpd and bootptab.

boot diskette   **Installation on the client**   First create a boot diskette as described
above. Then restart the computer on which **Linux Universe** is to be
installed with the boot diskette. Before you can boot successfully, you
might have to provide Linux with additional information on your the
boot options   hardware configuration. These boot options must be specified in the
boot manager. A list of possible boot options starts on page 54, and
a detailed description of the boot manager starts on page 76. After
booting, Linux will prompt you for the location of the installation
CD:

```
Device name of CD-ROM or <Enter> for automatic search: ?
Where is the Linux Universe runtime CD-ROM?
NFS location (in the form 192.1.0.18:/dist): 193.168.1.2:/dist
What is your Internet address?
Internet address: 193.168.1.4
What is your Network mask?
Network mask [255.255.255.0]: 255.255.255.0█
```

Figure 5.2.   Boot message

For manual NFS installation, enter 7 for nfs. For PLIP,
depending on the port used, choose 19, 20, or 21. For BOOTP
specify 22.

IP address   Next, for nfs or plipX you must enter the Internet address of
the server, followed by a colon, and the directory /dist.

Finally, you must specify the IP address of the computer on

which Linux is to be installed and the associated network mask.

For BOOTP these previous steps are not necessary. If the connection has been established successfully, you can proceed directly to the installation program.

5.3   Partitioning

If possible, you should create two, and ideally three, partitions for Linux: one for the file system (the root partition), which should encompass at least 100 MB if possible, and one swap partition. The third partition optionally allows physically separating user files from the operating system. Complete installation of the distribution requires 650 MB.

file system

swap

The swap partition is exclusively for temporary storage of regions of main memory that are presently not needed and, especially if your system has only 8 MB of RAM, should be dimensioned adequately. As a guideline, the swap partition plus the memory should total 16 MB, although 32 MB is better. Alternatively (or additionally) to a swap partition, you can create a swap file as described below.

swap file

The additional third partition contains the user's home directories, i.e., user-created files. The advantage here is that user files are physically decoupled from the operating system partition. This makes user files secure even in the event of an upgrade or reinstallation of the operating system partition. The dimension of this partition naturally depends on your needs, but 100 to 200 MB normally suffices.

Since the size of a partition cannot be changed later and dimensioning partitions demands some experience, we recommend that novices begin with one large partition for Linux.

The following applies **fundamentally** for hard-disk partitioning:

- Back up your files before you modify the partition table!
- Use the [p] command (option **Sectors**) of fdisk to display the partition table and record the partition information. This table can be your saving grace in the event of an error during partitioning; with this information and some luck, you can reconstruct the partition table.

33

- Changing a partition destroys all data on it!
- Carefully consider the dimensioning of the individual partitions, since the size cannot be changed easily later. Plan ahead.
- After modifying the partition table, restart your computer before taking any further steps!

primary partitions

To boot Linux directly, it must be installed on a primary partition. A hard disk can be divided into up to four primary partitions.

The restriction to primary partitions does not apply if you use the OS/2 boot manager. Regardless of the boot manager used, the Linux boot partition must principally reside within the first 1024 cylinders of the hard disk. This restriction applies because Linux is booted using a BIOS function that can only access the first 1024 cylinders.

extended and
logical partitions

If you need more partitions, then instead of a primary partition you must create an extended partition. An extended partition contains all the storage space that is not used by the primary partitions. On this extended partition you can then set up any number of logical partitions. Note that you cannot boot from logical partitions.

➡ *If an extended partition is deleted, this deletes all of the logical partitions on it and their data!*

The various partition types have different prerequisites for their creation:

Primary partition
There must be at most three existing primary partitions, or two primary and one extended partition. In addition, sectors must be free beyond these partitions.

Extended partition
There must be at most three primary partitions and no extended partition yet on the remaining hard disk.

Logical partition
The extended partition must still have free sectors.

If your hard disk lacks space for another partition, you can use the DOS program FIPS.EXE (see below) to split a DOS partition and thus create space for a new partition. On the other hand, if you still have space on your hard disk that has not been allocated to any partition, you can partition from the installation program, which invokes the Linux program `fdisk`.

As an alternative to `fdisk`, you can use the command-line-oriented version `lfdisk` under Linux. If you do not use these programs from within the installation program and you have multiple hard disks, the hard disk to be partitioned must be passed as a parameter, for example:

`fdisk /dev/hdb` for the second EIDE disk or
`fdisk /dev/sda` for the first SCSI disk.

```
                        cfdisk 0.8d BETA (>2GB)

                          Disk Drive: /dev/sda
             Heads: 64   Sectors per Track: 32   Cylinders: 1013

   Name        Flags       Part Type    FS Type              Size (MB)
------------------------------------------------------------------------
  /dev/sda1                Primary      DOS 16-bit >=32Mb       225.00
  /dev/sda2                Primary      Linux                    80.00
  /dev/sda3     Boot       Primary      Linux                   376.00
  /dev/sda5                Logical      Linux                   300.00
  /dev/sda6                Logical      Linux Swap               32.00




    [Bootable]  [ Delete ]   [ Help  ]  [Maximize]  [ Print ]
    [ Quit  ]   [ Type  ]   [ Units ]  [ Write  ]  [ X MBB ]

          Toggle bootable flag of the current partition
```

Figure 5.3.   fdisk

`fdisk` recognizes the following commands:

b (bootable flag) activates a partition. If you mark multiple partitions as active, Linux boots from the first active partition!

d deletes a partition

h displays explanations of individual commands

n creates a new partition

q terminates `fdisk` without changes

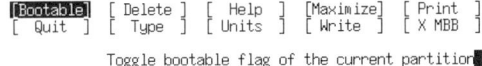

t specifies the partition type (default is `83`–Linux native). For swap partitions, use `82`.

W writes the partition table after confirmation with `yes`. Responding `no` terminates `fdisk` without changes.

35

> *Always restart your computer after any modification of the partition table!*

Splitting a DOS partition   The program FIPS.EXE, located in the root directory of the CD, enables splitting an existing DOS partition without data loss. Before creating a new partition, it tests whether there are files on the respective sectors. If so, FIPS.EXE aborts. In addition, you can abort FIPS.EXE at any time with `Ctrl` + `C`. FIPS enters the new partition at the end of the partition table, so that partitions beyond the split are not shifted in position. Thus FIPS does not affect the assignment of drive letters under DOS/95/NT or the device files under Linux. Also read the notes in the file FIPS09.DOC in the root directory of the installation CD.

You might need to optimize the DOS partition first with the DOS program DEFRAG.EXE in order to enable splitting at all. After optimization all files occupy contiguous blocks at the start of the partition, whereby the new partition can be allocated at the end of the existing partition.

Creating a swap file   If you lack sufficient space on your hard disk for a swap partition or if you temporarily need more swap space, Linux can employ a file instead of a partition as its swap space. *swap file size* Swap files have the advantage that their size can be varied at will. A swap file /swapfile of 16MB is created with the following command sequence:

```
dd if=/dev/zero of=/swapfile bs=1k count=16384
mkswap /swapdfile
sync
```

To activate the swap file on booting, you must enter the following line in the file /etc/fstab:

```
/swapfile none swap defaults 0 0
```

activate and deactivate However, you can also activate and deactivate both swap partitions and swap files at run time. Do this with the commands swapon and swapoff. In this example the swap file was activated with swapon /swapfile.

## Chapter 6

The installation program

Now you can progress sequentially through the steps of the installation program. Naturally it is possible to abort the installation program with the command **Quit**. Move the cursor with the cursor keys or with ⊞ and ⊟ to the desired menu item and then select it with ⌐Enter⌐ or ⌐Space⌐. ⌐Esc⌐ aborts any dialog.

After completion of the installation, the installation program can be re-invoked as needed under the login `root` with `install-menu`.

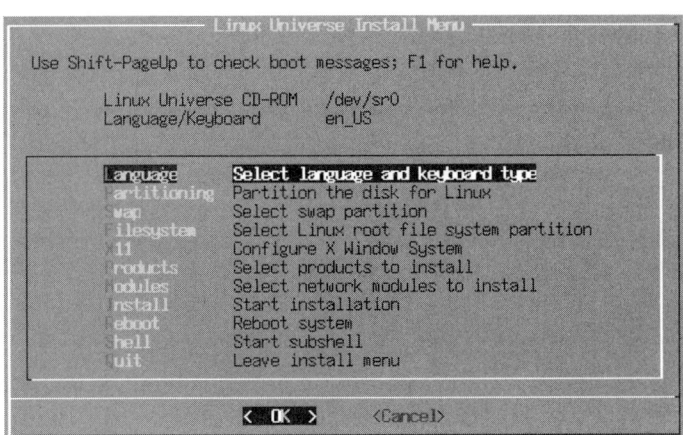

Figure 6.1. Installation—main menu

6.1 Language

First, select the language and keyboard layout of choice:

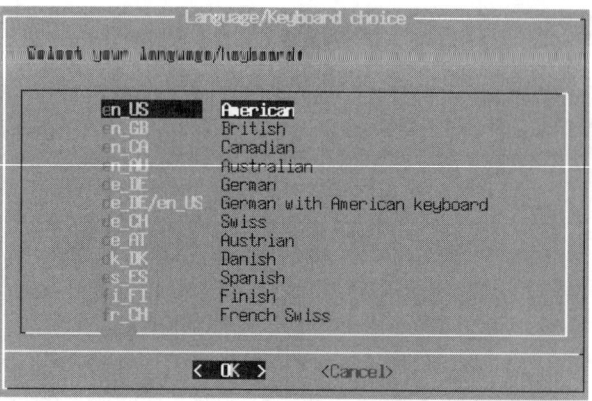

Figure 6.2. Language and keyboard

6.2 Partitioning

If you have not created a partition for Linux yet, you can do so now. Execute the menu item **partitioning** even if you have created a partition for Linux with the FDISK program in DOS. In this case you still need to set the correct partition type for the Linux partitions: select the menu item **Fdisk**. After launching fdisk, you can specify the partition type with $\boxed{t}$.

Figure 6.3. Setting the partition type

At the subsequent prompt you need to enter 83 for Linux (the default) or 82 for Linux swap.

Read the section on partitioning (starting on page 33) before ◀
you continue!!!

Figure 6.4. Partitioning

If you want to install the **Linux Universe** master boot record,
then after selecting **boot block** you must still specify on which
physical hard disk the master boot record is to be installed.

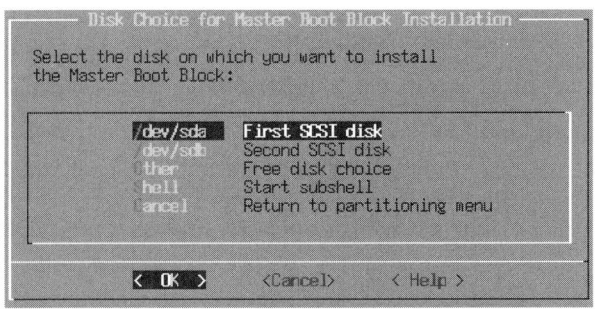

Figure 6.5. Boot record installation

Under the option **Fdisk** you must specify which physical hard
disk you want to partition. (See Figure 6.6.)

Next, the program `fdisk` is invoked; it is described in more
detail beginning on page 33. After this program terminates, you return
to the installation program.

If you have modified the partition table, then you must restart
the system. (See Figure 6.7.)

39

Figure 6.6. Selecting the hard disk

6.3 Swap partition

Now you can select the swap partition. (See Figure 6.8.)

Other lets you select from among all available partitions. (See Figure 6.9.)

Finally, you need to initialize and activate the swap partition. If you leave the swap partition deactivated, it is created but not used by the system. A deactivated swap partition can be activated manually later (see page 33). (See Figure 6.10.)

6.4 File system partition

Selecting the partition for the file system is completely analogous. This is the partition where Linux is installed. Under the menu item

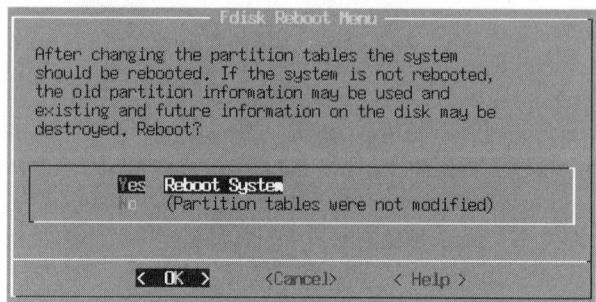

Figure 6.7. Restart

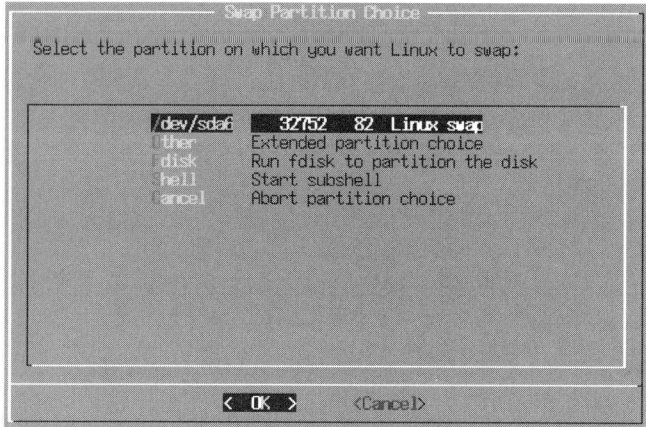

Figure 6.8. Swap partition

Other you will also find DOS partitions listed. If you specify a DOS
partition here, Linux is installed in the directory \LINUX of the DOS
partition. (See Figure 6.11.)

If you want to use more than one partition for the file system,
such as with a second partition for users' home directories, then
execute the menu item **Filesystem** repeatedly. For the additional

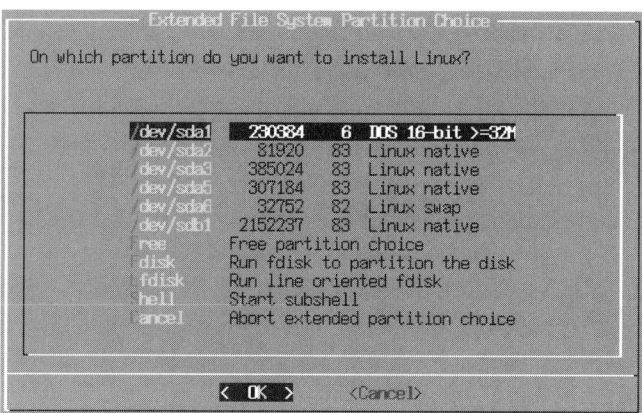

Figure 6.9. Extended choice

41

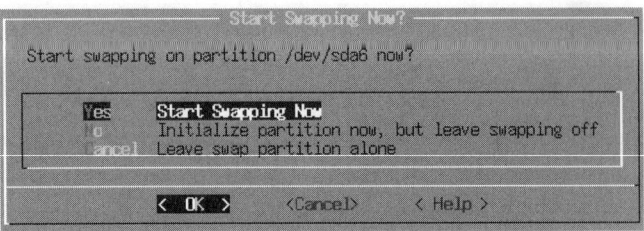

Figure 6.10. Activating the swap partition

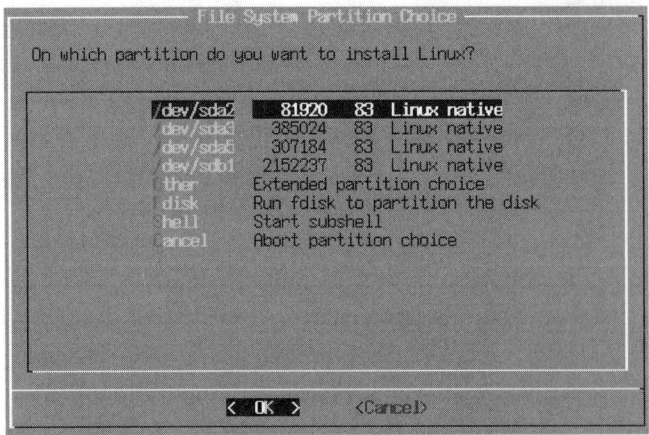

Figure 6.11. File system partition

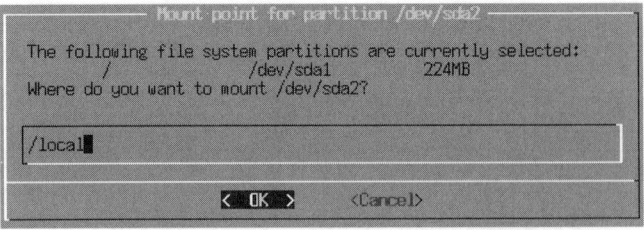

Figure 6.12. Target directory for mounting

partitions, the program prompts for the target directory for mounting (or mount-point). (See Figure 6.12.)

To deselect a partition, leave the entry field blank and press [Enter]. This also applies to the root partition, which always has the directory / as its mount-point.

The selected partitions and their mount-points are displayed in the head of the main menu.

6.5   X11 configuration

Here you can make settings required for the installation of the X-Window system (called X11). If you have difficulties with the hardware of your system, read the files /etc/XF86Config and /usr/doc/howto/XFree86-HOWTO.gz; due to the multitude of different hardware components, we cannot handle individual configurations here. To change the X11 configuration later, invoke the configuration program under the login root with ConfigXF86. (See Figure 6.13.)

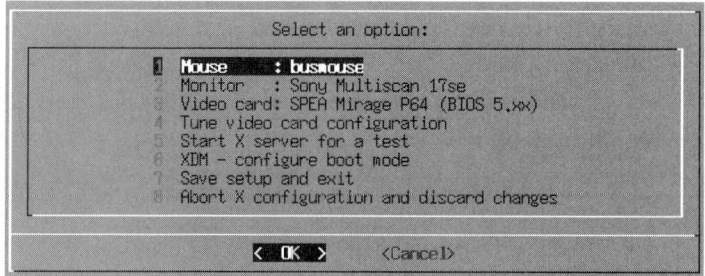

Figure 6.13.   X11 configuration

Mouse

First you must specify the type of your mouse. *If you have a bus mouse, observe the instructions on page 69 under bus mice!* (See Figure 6.14.)

Next you must specify whether your mouse has two or three buttons. (See Figure 6.15.)

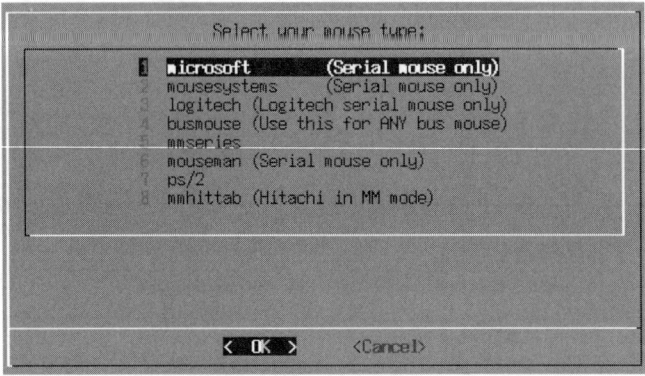

Figure 6.14. Mouse type

Next you must specify the port where your mouse is connected. (See Figure 6.16.) The following entries are possible:

default	first serial port
/dev/ttyS0	serial mouse at first serial port
/dev/ttyS1	serial mouse at second serial port
/dev/logibm	Logitec bus mouse
/dev/inportbm	Microsoft bus mouse
/dev/psaux	PS/2 bus mouse, frequent for laptops (notebooks) and on-board bus mice
/dev/atibm	ATI-XL bus mouse

In exceptional cases, the last menu option lets you select the mouse port freely. (See Figure 6.17.)

Finally, you will be prompted for confirmation. (See Figure 6.18.)

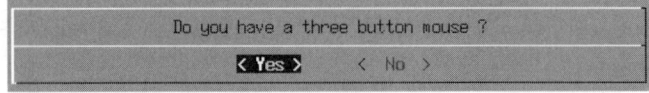

Figure 6.15. Number of buttons

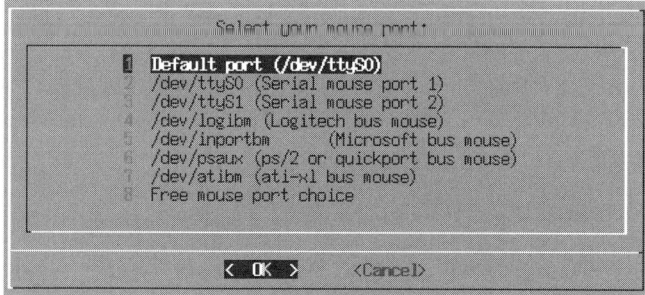

Figure 6.16. Mouse port

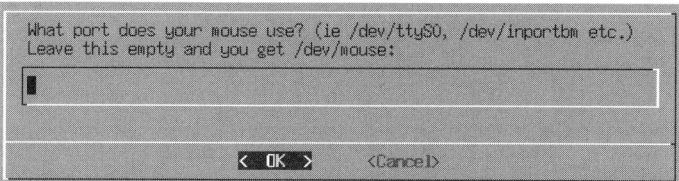

Figure 6.17. Free choice of the mouse port

Monitor

Now use the cursor keys or ⊕ and ⊖ to select the monitor. This is the most delicate point in the X-Window installation, since using a driver that is incompatible with the monitor can seriously damage the latter! *If your monitor behaves strangely on starting the X-server, or if it flutters or displays a distorted picture, immediately press*

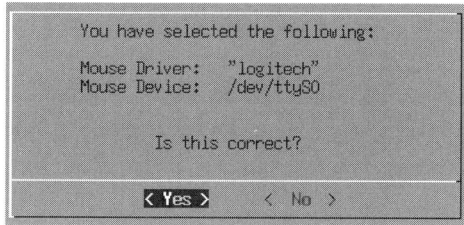

Figure 6.18. Confirmation

45

$\boxed{\text{Ctrl}}+\boxed{\text{Alt}}+\boxed{\text{Backspace}}$ *to abort the X-server, or* $\boxed{\text{Ctrl}}+\boxed{\text{Alt}}+\boxed{\text{F1}}$ *to switch to text mode.*

In case of doubt, select the **VESA generic monitor**. This all-around driver can be adapted later to your device. (See Figure 6.19.)

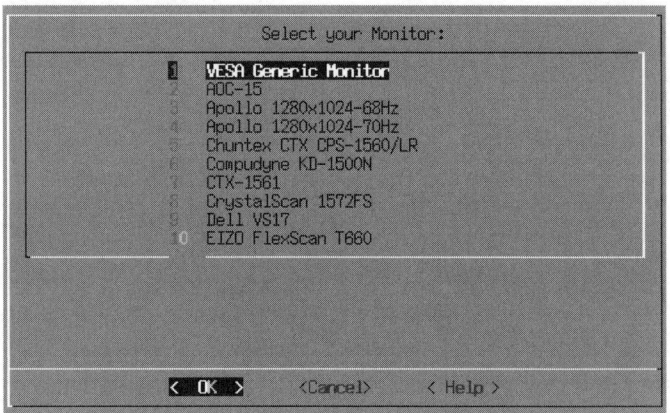

Figure 6.19. Monitor

Video adapter

Next select your video adapter, or the one that comes closest, from the list of video adapters. In case of doubt, choose the generic driver. (See Figure 6.20.)

Optimizing video configuration

Here we will attempt to determine the sync rate of your video adapter. This test is not absolutely necessary. (See Figure 6.21.)

Testing the X-server

Patience!

Here you can test whether the settings you made support your hardware correctly. After you invoke this menu item, you might have to wait several minutes until the test screen appears, since at this point the file cache is not active yet and the corresponding X-server must first be built up. For later operation the X-server is transferred from the CD to the hard disk and thus starts significantly faster. The test

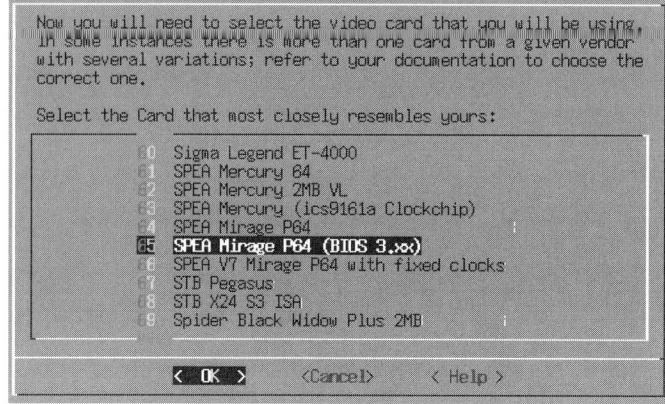

Figure 6.20. Video adapter

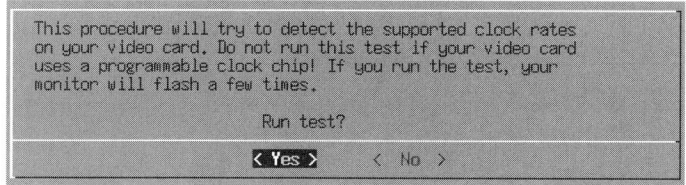

Figure 6.21. Optimizing

screen consists of a black and white grid with a black cross as cursor.
End the test with Ctrl + Alt + Backspace. (See Figure 6.22.)

When you start the X-server, if your monitor behaves strangely, ◀
flutters, or displays a distorted picture, immediately press Ctrl +
Alt + Backspace, *to abort the X-server!*

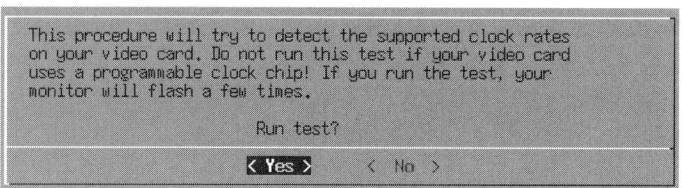

Figure 6.22. Testing the X-server

47

You can change the resolution with [Ctrl] + [Alt] + [+] or [Ctrl] + [Alt] + [−] on the numeric keypad.

If the cursor does not move or only jumps to a corner, you need a different driver, a different path, or, for a bus mouse, possibly a different interrupt for booting.

XDM configuration

graphical login

Here you can enable the automatic start of the X-Window system after booting; X-Window presents itself with a graphical login. Alternatively, you can launch X-Window from the command line with startx. (See Figure 6.23.)

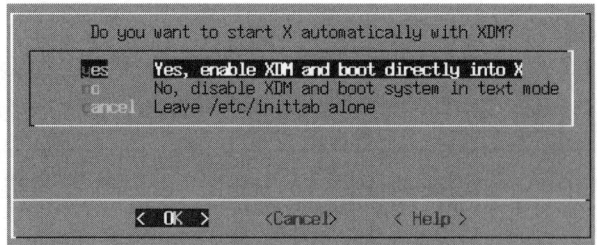

Figure 6.23. Booting

6.6 Products

Here you can select the packages to be installed from the beginning. (See Figure 6.24.)

6.7 Network adapter selection

If your system has a network adapter, this is where you specify the model. (See Figure 6.25.)

6.8 Installation

This menu item initiates the actual installation. The Linux base system of about 30 MB and the packages selected under **Products** are copied onto your hard disk. If the file cache is activated, no other

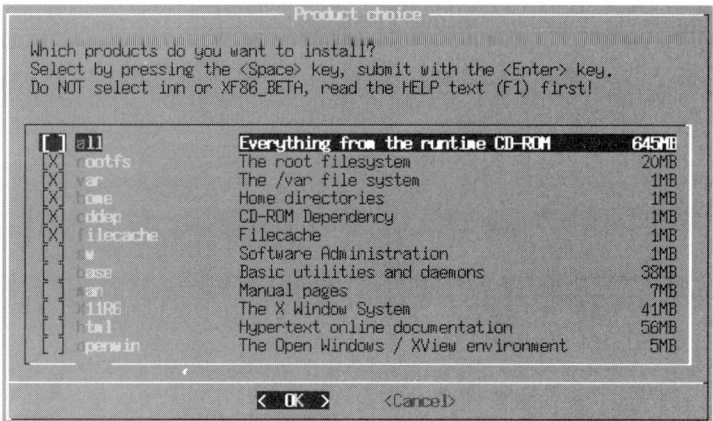

Figure 6.24. Package selection

application program, documentation, etc. is copied onto the hard disk until the respective file is invoked for the first time. Without file cache, the installation makes available only those packages selected under **Products**. Chapter 9, "Administration," describes how to install individual packages later.

Before the installation begins, the following dialog appears for each partition that already contains a file system (i.e., that is

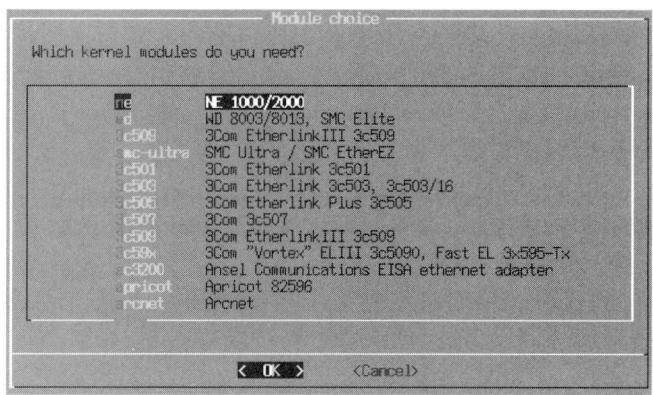

Figure 6.25. Module for the network adapter

formatted). The head of the dialog displays to which partition the prompt refers. (See Figure 6.26.)

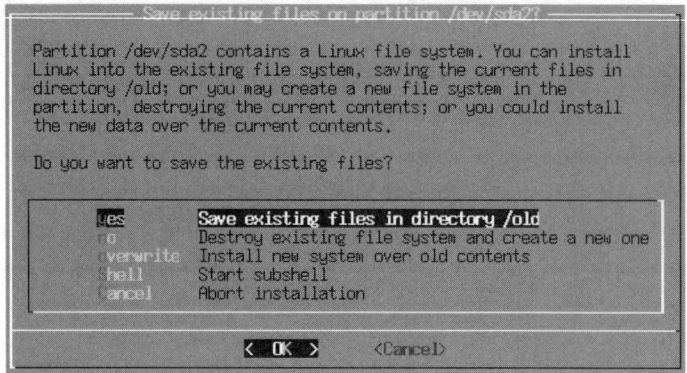

Figure 6.26. Saving or overwriting existing data

If you choose to save the data, the existing directory structure is saved in the directory /old (a second such save stores the data in /old/old). *If you choose the option* **no**, *the existing file system is not saved. The corresponding partition is reformatted, which destroys all existing data on it!* The option **overwrite** mounts the partition to its mount-point without formatting it first; then the system is installed over the old partition contents. However, a partition mounted to /local remains untouched, since the installation program copies no files into this directory or its subdirectories.

On the other hand, if you have chosen a DOS partition as your root partition, you can install Linux there in the directory \LINUX. (See Figure 6.27.)

Alternatively, you can create a Linux file system on the DOS partition. *This destroys all data on the DOS partition because the partition is reformatted!*

6.9   Reboot

After successful installation or repartitioning, you need to reboot the system. If you used a boot diskette and completed the installation, do not forget to remove the diskette from the drive.

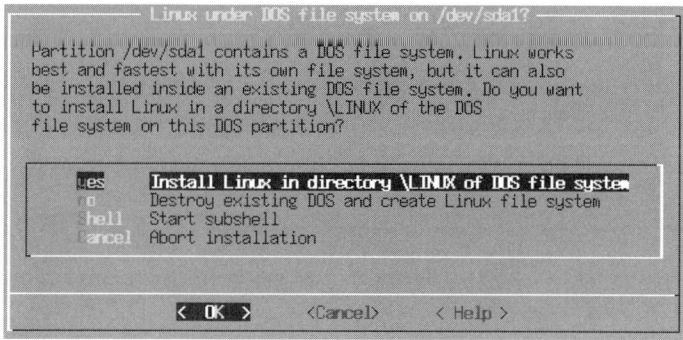

Figure 6.27. DOS partition

```
Starting subshell; type Control-D to return to install menu
Subshell # ▮
```

Figure 6.28. Launching the shell

6.10   Launching a shell

The menu item **Shell** launches a shell as a subprocess. Terminate the
shell by entering ⌈Ctrl⌉ + ⌈d⌉. (See Figure 6.28.)

6.11   Aborting installation

Quit aborts the installation program without any changes. Then a
shell is also launched. Before termination of the installation program,
you are prompted for confirmation. (See Figure 6.29.)

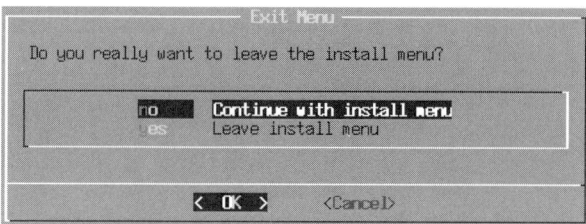

Figure 6.29. Quit

## Chapter 7

The boot system

7.1   Boot options

Boot options are parameters that are passed to the Linux kernel on booting. They are comparable to command line options of normal programs. They are specified in the boot manager or when starting Linux from DOS as parameters for INSTALL.EXE or LOADLIN.EXE.

Boot options serve to tell the operating system which drive and which partition to use as the root file system. In addition, you can pass more exact information on the hardware configuration to Linux.

On booting, each driver that was compiled into the kernel probes whether a certain device is present. If the device is found, support for it is activated. This automatic detection can go wrong, for example, if the device is on an unaccustomed interrupt. In such a case the driver can be informed explicitly via its boot option which interrupt the device uses. Additionally, the associated port number can also be specified. If autoprobing for a hardware component fails, the corresponding boot option needs to be specified.

Some drivers also permit switching off autoprobe. In rare cases this can be necessary, such as when a driver erroneously detects a device that is not present.

Because Linux is case-sensitive, the boot options must be specified exactly as follows.

Multiple boot options can be specified, delimited by blanks. Storage addresses are specified with at least five places; PC addresses are sometimes given in four digits, so add a leading zero as needed. Hexadecimal numbers always begin with 0x. Parameter values in square brackets ([]) are optional. We also refer you to the description of boot options in the file README in the root directory of the **Linux Universe CD.**

Root file system   This boot option allows you to specify the drive or partition that Linux is to regard as the root file system.

root=/dev/hdaN
> specifies the Nth partition of the first IDE/EIDE hard disk
> (e.g., /dev/hda2 for the second partition)

root=/dev/hdbN
> specifies the Nth partition of the second IDE/EIDE hard disk
> (e.g., /dev/hdb1 for the first partition)

root=/dev/sdaN
> specifies the Nth partition of the first SCSI hard disk
> (e.g., /dev/sda1 for the first partition), and analogously
> /dev/sdbN for the second SCSI hard disk

root=/dev/sr0
> for the first SCSI CD-ROM

root=/dev/sr1
> for the second SCSI CD-ROM

root=/dev/hda
> for an EIDE/ATAPI CD-ROM that is connected as master to
> the first controller

root=/dev/hdb
> for an EIDE/ATAPI CD-ROM that is connected as slave to
> the first controller

root=/dev/hdc
> for an EIDE/ATAPI CD-ROM that is connected as master to
> the second controller

root=/dev/hdd
> for an EIDE/ATAPI CD-ROM that is connected as slave to
> the second controller

root=/dev/mcd
> for a non-EIDE/ATAPI CD-ROM by Mitsumi

root=/dev/sbpcd
> for a Kotobuki/Matsushita/Panasonic CD-ROM, model
> CR-521/522/523/562/563

root=/dev/cdu535

for a Sony CDU-535/531 CD-ROM

root=/dev/cm206cd

for a Laser-Magnetic Storage drive model CM-206 by Philips

root=/dev/gscd

for a Goldstar R420 CD-ROM

root=/dev/aztcd

for Aztech CDA-268-01A, Orchid CD-3110, Okano
CDD110, Wearnes CDD110

root=/dev/sonycd

for Sony CDU-31A or CDU-33A

root=/dev/sjcd

for a Sanyo CDR-H94A CD-ROM

root=/dev/fd0

specifies the first floppy disk drive

root=/dev/fd1

specifies the second floppy disk drive

root=0B01

specifies a device with major device number `0x0B`
(decimal 11) and minor device number `0x01`. This example
corresponds to `/dev/sr1`

Note: If only one device is connected to an IDE/EIDE controller,
it must be configured as master and addressed as `/dev/hda` or
`/dev/hdc`.

Furthermore, for the root file system one of the following mount
options can be specified:

ro causes the root file system to be mounted as read-only during
booting. This is necessary in order to carry out checks on the
file system. After booting, the file system is automatically
released for writing.

rw permits read and write operations from the beginning.

Boot messages

debug

specifies messages

This enables the display of detailed messages during booting.

Selecting the CD-ROM driver   Meanwhile the standard kernel contains many drivers for non-IDE/EIDE/ATAPI/SCSI drives that can cause conflicts during booting. This option permits specifying a certain driver, thus disabling all other drivers. In addition to this option, you might also need to use the option of the corresponding drive.

cdrom=type

>   specifies a certain type of drive, where valid values for **type** are:

>>   **isp16** for a CD-ROM on an ISP16 sound card

>>   **spbcd** for a CD-ROM on another sound card

>>   **cdu31a** for a Sony CDU-31A or CDU-33A CD-ROM

>>   **aztcd** for an Aztech CD-ROM

>>   **mcd** for a Mitsumi CD-ROM

>>   **mcdx** experimental driver for Mitsumi

>>   **sonycd535** for a Sony CDU-535/531 CD-ROM

>>   **gscd** for a GoldStar R420 CD-ROM

>>   **cm206** for a Philips CM-206 CD-ROM

>>   **optcd** for an Optics Storage 8000 AT CD-ROM

>>   **sjcd** for a Sanyo CDR-H94A CD-ROM

>>   **none** disables the drivers of all non-IDE/EIDE/ATAPI/SCSI drives

>>   **debug** displays a message during autoprobing of each driver

Examples

```
cdrom=mcd
```

activates only the driver for Mitsumi CD-ROM drives

```
cdrom=sbpcd,mcd
```

activates only the driver for Mitsumi and SoundBlaster CD-ROM drives

```
cdrom=mcd mcd=0x300,10
```

selects a driver and sets one option for the driver

SCSI adapter Analogously to the `cdrom` option, you can use the option `scsi` to select a SCSI adapter. This, too, deactivates all other drivers. If the driver itself must be configured, use the boot option of the corresponding adapter.

scsi=type

> specifies a SCSI controller, where valid values for **type** are: `advansys`, `aha152x`, `aha1542`, `aha174x`, `aic7xxx`, `AM53C974`, `BusLogic`, `dtc3x80`, `eata`, `eata_dma`, `eata_pio`, `fdomain`, `in2000`, `ncr5380`, `ncr53c406a`, `ncr53c7xx`, `ncr53c8xx`, `pas16`, `ppa`, `qlogicfas`, `qlogicisp`, `st0x`, `t128`, `tmc8xx`, `u14_34`, `ultrastor`, `wd7000`

scsi=none

> disables the drivers of all SCSI adapters

scsi=debug

> displays a message on autoprobing each driver

Examples

>   scsi=aic7xxx

disables all drivers except `aic7xxx`

>   scsi=aic7xxx,aha1542

disables all drivers except `aic7xxx` and `aha1542`

>   scsi=aic7xxx aic7xxx=extended

selects a driver and sets an option for the driver

Input/output This option allows you to reserve certain ports; this means that the system does not look for devices in the specified regions and suppresses autoprobing. This can be necessary if you use other boot options to assign hardware components to certain ports.

reserve=address,number[,address,number]

> reserves `number` ports beginning at `address` inclusively. Multiple regions can be specified, delimited by commas

Example

```
reserve=0x300,0x10,0x320,0x10
```

reserves the ports `0x300` to `0x30F` and `0x320` to `0x32F`

RAM-disk   A RAM-disk is used primarily for initial installation, since at that time there is no hard disk file system yet. After booting, the RAM-disk can be accessed under `/dev/ramdisk`.

ramdisk_size=N

> effects the installation of a RAM-disk with `N` kilobytes; this option replaces the old `ramdisk` boot option

ramdisk_start=N

> specifies a RAM-disk image on a diskette beginning at offset `N` sectors

prompt_ramdisk={0,1}

> `1` provides a chance to change diskettes before loading begins; `0` reads from the current diskette without confirmation

load_ramdisk={0,1}

> `1` effects loading of a RAM-disk image from diskette; `0` suppresses this

RAM-disk image   With this option the operating system reads an image of a RAM-disk from the boot diskette. This requires specifying an offset for where the image is located on the diskette. Then the RAM-disk is mounted as root file system.

cram=N

> reads a compressed RAM-disk image from the diskette starting at offset `N` (e.g., for `cram=800` at 800 KB)

Main memory   This option tells Linux how much main memory (RAM) to use. Specifying this option is necessary if your computer has more than 64 MB of RAM. The following examples all specify 80 MB of RAM:

`mem=0x5000000`	hexadecimal specification
`mem=80M`	specification in megabytes
`mem=81920K`	specification in kilobytes
`mem=83886080`	specification in bytes

Pentium kernel on 486 machines   This option is necessary if a Pentium-optimized kernel is to be booted on a 486 machine.

mem=nopentium disables Pentium extension in memory
                      management

Coprocessor   Some coprocessors run only in real mode and crash under Linux. This option disables the coprocessor and employs floating-point emulation. This requires recompilation of the kernel.

no387 disables the coprocessor

Halt instruction   If your processor has problems with the HALT machine instruction, you need to employ this option:

no-hlt prevents use of the HALT instruction

SCSI LUNs   This option restricts the LUNs (logical unit numbers) where Linux probes for devices. This is necessary if SCSI devices are found more than once or to support CD changers. In both cases the kernel must be recompiled so that it supports multiple LUNs.

max_scsi_luns=N causes only the first N LUNs to be tested

Example

    max_scsi_luns=1

ignores all SCSI LUNs except the first

SCSI streamer buffer   This allows you to set the buffer size for a SCSI streamer.

st=N,M creates N buffers of 1024 bytes each and triggers writing
           when the first M buffers are full

Example

    st=128,64

Adaptec AHA152X/1505/1515-SCSI adapter

aha152x=address,interrupt,SCSI ID,reconnect,parity
         specifies the address, the interrupt, and the SCSI ID.
         reconnect and parity can assume values 0 or 1 (on/off)

59

Example

```
aha152x=0x320,11,7,1,1
```

sets the address to `0x320`, the interrupt to `11`, and the SCSI ID to `7`, and enables reconnect and parity

Adaptec AHA1540/1542 SCSI adapter

aha1542=address[bus-on,bus-off,DMA]
specifies the `address`; optional parameters: `bus-on` and `bus-off` interval as well as DMA rate. The `bus-on` interval can be specified in the range 2-15 μs, the `bus-off` interval 1-64 μs. DMA rate accepts the values 5, 6, 7, 8, or 10 MB/s.

Examples

```
aha1542=0x334
```

sets address `0x334`

```
aha1542=0x334,11,4,5
```

sets address `0x334`, bus-on interval `11` μs, bus-off interval `4` μs, and DMA rate `5` MB/s

Adaptec AHA274x/2842/294x/39xx-AIC 7xxx SCSI adapter   The Adaptec AHA-2920 is not set via this boot option, but via the Future Domain driver (see page 63).

aic7xxx=extended
forces reordering of the BIOS geometry. This is necessary if the connected hard disks are larger than 1 GB. Caution: *Changing this option requires repartitioning!*

aic7xxx=no_reset
Some SCSI devices require a certain waiting time after resetting the bus. This option turns off the waiting time.

AdvanSys SCSI controller   This option permits specification of ports where the driver should probe for an Advansys adapter. This affects only ISA/VLB boards.

advansys=[address1[,address2[,address3[,address4]]]]
> restricts probing for an AdvanSys adapter to at most four
> addresses.

Examples

```
advansys=0x0
```

suppresses probing for an AdvanSys controller

```
advansys=0x110,0x210,0x230,0x330
```

restricts probing to the four specified ports

Always IN2000 SCSI adapter

```
in2000=ioport:address,noreset,period:N,disconnect:M
```
> The parameters can be specified individually or in any
> combination. A parameter must be separated from its value by
> a colon without a blank. The parameters mean the following:
> ```
> ioport:address
> ```
>> specifies an IN200 controller at a certain `address`
> ```
> noreset
> ```
>> no reset of the SCSI bus on booting
> ```
> period:N
> ```
>> minimal duration of SCSI data transfers in nanoseconds
>> (range: 250-1000)
> ```
> disconnect:M
> ```
>> 0: no disconnects, 1: variable disconnects, 2:
>> disconnects enabled

Example

```
in2000=ioport:0x220,noreset
```

specifies address `0x220` and disables bus-reset `in2000=period:`
`250,disconnect:2`

AM53/79C974 SCSI adapter   This driver enables varying several
transfer parameters between the adapter and a SCSI device.

AM53C974=host-ID,device-ID,max-rate,max-offset
specifies a maximum transfer rate of `max-rate` MHz
(3..10) with an offset of `max-offset` bytes (0..15) for
communication between the adapter with the SCSI ID
`host-ID` and the device with ID `device-ID`

Example

```
AM53C974=7,1,10,0
```

specifies a transfer rate of `10` MHz between the adapter with ID `7`
and the device with the ID `1`, with no offset.

BusLogic SCSI adapter Due to the compatibility of many
BusLogic adapters with Adaptec adapters, the former also run with
the `aha1542` driver, with which you sometimes get better results.

`buslogic=address`
specifies a certain `address`. Specifying `0` suppresses
probing for a BusLogic adapter.

Examples

```
buslogic=0x334
```

specifies a BusLogic adapter at address `0x334`

```
buslogic=NoProbe
```

suppresses probing for a BusLogic adapter

EATA SCSI adapter

`eata=address`
specifies a certain `address`. Specifying `noprobe` disables
the adapter.

Example

```
eata=0x230
```

EATA PM2011B/9X / PM2021A/9X / PM2012A / PM2012B / PM2022A/9X / PM2122A/9X / PM2322A/9X SCSI adapter

`eata_dma=address`
>   specifies a certain `address`. Specifying `noprobe` disables the adapter.

Example

```
eata_dma=0x230
```

EATA DPT PM2001 SCSI adapter

`eata_pio=address`
>   specifies a certain `address`. Specifying `noprobe` disables the adapter.

Example

```
eata_pio=0x170
```

Future Domain TMC-8xx/TMC-950 SCSI adapter

`tmc8xx=address,interrupt`
>   specifies a TMC-8xx/TMC-950 controller at a certain `address` and a certain `interrupt`.

Example

```
tmc8xx=0xc80000,15
```

specifies address `0xc80000` and interrupt `15`

Future Domain TMC-16x0/TMC-3260/Adaptec AHA2920 SCSI adapter

`fdomain=address[,interrupt,adapter-ID]`
>   specifies the `address` and the `interrupt`. Optionally, the SCSI ID of the adapter can be specified.

Example

```
fdomain=0x140,12,7
```

specifies address `0x140`, the IRQ `12`, and the SCSI ID `7`

63

NCR-5380 SCSI adapter

ncr5380=address,interrupt[,DMA channel]
    specifies the address and the interrupt. Optionally, the
    DMA channel can be specified.

Examples

    ncr5380=0xcc000,5

    ncr5380=0xcc000,5,6

    ncr5380=0xcc000,255,255

disables interrupt and DMA

NCR-53C400 SCSI adapter

ncr53c400=address,interrupt
    specifies the address and the interrupt

Examples

    ncr53c400=0xcc000,5

specifies address 0xcc000 and interrupt 5

    ncr53c400=0xcc000,255

specifies address 0xcc000 and operation without interrupt

    ncr53c400=0xcc000,254

specifies address 0xcc000 and self-recognition of interrupts

    ncr53c400=0,255

disables the adapter

NCR-53C406A SCSI adapter

ncr53c406a=address[,interrupt[,PIO-mode]]
    specifies a certain address. Optionally, the interrupt
    and the PIO mode can be specified: 0 slow, 1 fast.

Example

    ncr53c406a=0x300

specifies address `0x300`

```
ncr53c406a=0
```

non-interrupt-based operating mode

Pro Audio Spectrum 16 SCSI adapter

`pas16=address,interrupt`
  specifies the `address` and the `interrupt`

Examples

```
pas16=0x388,10
```

specifies address `0x388` and interrupt `10`

```
pas16=0x388,255
```

disables interrupt

Seagate ST01/ST02 controller

`st0x=address,interrupt`
  specifies an ST01/ST02 controller at a certain `address` and
  `interrupt`

Example

```
st0x=0xc80000,15
```

specifies address `0xc80000` and interrupt `15`

Trantor T128/T128F/T228 SCSI adapter

`t128=address,interrupt`
  specifies a Trantor controller at a certain `address` and an
  `interrupt`

Example

```
t128=0xcc000,5
```

Ultrastor 14F/24F/34F adapter

`us14f=address[,address]`
  specifies a certain `address`. Optionally, the address of a
  second adapter can be specified.

Examples

```
us14_34=0x330
```

specifies an Ultrastor adapter at address `0x330`

```
us14_34=0x330,0x340
```

specifies two Ultrastor adapters

WD7000 SCSI adapter

`wd7000=interrupt,DMA`
  specifies a certain `address` and a DMA channel

Example

```
wd7000=15,6
```

specifies interrupt `15` and DMA channel `6`

Printer (parallel port) With this option you can specify the interrupts and the parallel ports that the printer driver within the kernel uses. By default the driver uses all parallel ports. This option enables assigning only certain ports to the printer driver. When this option is used, only the ports specified are used by the driver. All other ports are not registered by the driver.

`lp=address0[,IRQ0[,address1[,IRQ1[,address2[,IRQ2]]]]]`
  specifies the addresses and interrupts of up to three parallel ports. The value `0` for the interrupt causes the driver not to use the respective port.

Examples

```
lp=0x278,5,0x378,7
```

specifies the first parallel port at address `0x278` and interrupt `5`, and the second parallel port at address `0x378` and interrupt `7`

```
lp=0
```

deactivates the driver

IOMEGA ZIP100 on a parallel port (non-SCSI version)

`ppa=address[,speed_high[,speed_low[,nybble]]]`
    specifies a ZIP-drive at a certain `address`. Optional
    parameters are:
    `speed_high` number of microseconds used for data
                transfer
    `speed_low` number of microseconds used for other
                operations
    `nybble` 0: 8-bit mode; 1: 4-bit mode

Note: For this driver to function, it must not use the same parallel
ports as the printer driver. By default the printer driver uses all ports,
which necessitates using the `lp` boot option.

Examples

    `ppa=0x378,0,3`

specifies a ZIP-drive on the first parallel port without data transfer
delay and 3 microseconds delay for other operations

    `lp=0x378 ppa=0x278`

ensures that the first parallel port is used for the printer and the second
for the ZIP drive

Baycom Radio Modem

`baycom=type,address,IRQ,option`
    specifies a Baycom-Modem. For more detailed information,
    see the kernel source code under `drivers/char`

Example

    `baycom=1,0x3f8,3,1`

specifies a Baycom-Modem of type ser12 at address `0x3f8` on
interrupt 3 with software DCD

RISCom/8 serial port adapter

`riscom8=address1[,address2[...]`
    specifies the addresses of up to four RISCom/8 adapters

Ethernet interfaces   With this option you can set the parameters of Ethernet interfaces.

`ether=IRQ,address,[start,end,]port`
>   specifies the interrupt `IRQ` and the `address` of a `port`. Optionally, you can specify the memory region to be used with `start` and `end`.

Examples

>   `ether=15,0x280,eth0`

specifies interrupt `15` and I/O port `0x280` for the first ethernet interface (`eth0`)

>   `ether=15,0x280,0xcc000,0xcdfff,eth1`

specifies interrupt `15`, I/O port `0x280` and the memory region from `0xcc000` to `0xcdfff` for the second Ethernet interface (`eth1`)

Teles ISDN adapter   The Teles ISDN driver works only with EURO-ISDN or 1TR6 lines.

`teles=p0,i0,m0,d0[,p1,i1,m1,d1 ...`
>   `,pn,in,mn,dn]`
>   This driver supports up to 16 adapters. The following are the individual parameters:
>   p0   address of the first adapter (default: `0xd80`)
>   i0   interrupt of the first adapter (default: `15`)
>   m0   memory region of the first adapter (default: `0xd0000`)
>   d0   D channel protocol of the first adapter: 1 for 1TR6, 2 for EDSS1 (default)

The parameters for the other adapters are specified analogously. See further information in the directory `/usr/src/linux/ Documentation/isdn`.

Example

>   `teles=0xd80,15,0x0d0000,2,teles1`

ICN ISDN adapters

```
icn=p,m[,idstring1[,idstring2]]
```
> specifies address p and a memory region at m. Optionally, you can set a name for the adapter. For the double ICN adapter, you must specify two names.

See `/usr/src/linux/Documentation/isdn` for more information.

Example

```
icn=0x340,0x0d0000,icn1,icn2
```

PCBIT-D ISDN adapters

```
pcbit=address[,interrupt[,...]
```
> enables specification of the addresses and the interrupts of up to four PCBIT ISDN adapters

Example

```
pcbit=0xD0000,5
```

Bus mice   These options allow you to specify the interrupt of your bus mouse.

```
bmouse=IRQ
```
> specifies a non-Microsoft bus mouse on interrupt IRQ
```
bmousems=IRQ
```
> specifies a Microsoft bus mouse on interrupt IRQ

Note: Specifying 0 as interrupt deactivates the respective bus mouse. Bus mice normally use interrupts 2, 3, 4, or 5, with the default being 5. The interrupt depends on the hardware configuration. For example, if your computer has two parallel as well as two serial ports, the bus mouse might be diverted to interrupt 9. Read the documentation for your bus mouse and the file `Busmouse-HOWTO.gz` in the directory `/usr/doc/howto`.

Examples

```
bmouse=5
```

specifies a non-Microsoft bus mouse on interrupt 5

```
bmousems=0
```

deactivates a Microsoft bus mouse

Floppy disk drives As a rule, floppy disk drives are fully recognized. For particular configurations the following options are available:

```
floppy=all_drives
```
>   probes for more than two drives per controller
```
floppy=daring
```
>   effects fastest and most efficient operation of the drives, but cannot be used with every controller
```
floppy=0,daring
```
>   effects slower but more secure operation
```
floppy=[address,]two_fdc
```
>   forces probing for a second controller; optionally, you can specify an `address`
```
thinkpad
```
>   for drives with transposed lines for changing diskettes
```
floppy=N,type,cmos
```
>   tells the system that the Nth floppy disk drive (starting at 0) is of a certain `type`. The following types can be specified:
>   >   0 unknown
>   >   1 5.25" DD drive
>   >   2 5.25" HD drive
>   >   3 3.5" DD drive
>   >   4 3.5" HD drive
>   >   5,6 3.5" ED drive
```
floppy=no_unexpected_interrupts
```
>   suppresses messages for unexpected interrupts

Example

```
floppy=0x370,two_fdc
```

probes at address 0x370 for a second controller

Mitsumi CD-ROM (non-EIDE/ATAPI) For operating multiple Mitsumi drives, there is an experimental driver named `mcdx`. See the kernel documentation in `Documentation/cdrom/mdcx`.

`mcd=address,interrupt`
> specifies a certain `address` and `interrupt`

Examples

    mcd=0

suppresses probing for a Mitsumi CD-ROM

    mcd=0x300,10

sets address `0x300` and interrupt `10`

Matsushita/Panasonic/Kotobuki CR-521/522/523/562/563 This option is necessary for operating CD-ROM drives that are on sound cards.

`sbpcd=address,type`
> specifies a certain `address` and the sound card type. The following types are available:
> `LaserMate`
>> SoundBlaster CD on a SoundBlaster-compatible sound card
>
> `SoundBlaster`
>> SoundBlaster CD on a SoundBlaster-Pro port
>
> `SPEA`
>> SoundBlaster CD on a SPEA-FX sound card

Examples

    sbpcd=0x230,SoundBlaster

Try this option if the address of the CD port is under 0x300.

    sbpcd=0x320,LaserMate

Try this option if the address of the CD port is over 0x300.

    sbpcd=0x330,SPEA

for SPEA sound cards

Aztech CD-ROM CDA-268-01A, Orchid CD-3110, Okano CDD110, Wearnes CDD110

```
atzcd=address[,0x79]
```
specifies the `address` of the CD drive. The optional parameter `0x79` forces recognition even if the firmware is not found.

Examples

```
aztcd=0
```

suppresses probing

```
aztcd=0x320,0x79
```

specifies address `0x320` and forces recognition

Sony CDU-31A or CDU-33A

Note: This driver makes no autoprobing. If you have one of these drives, you need to specify this option.

```
cdu31a=address,interrupt[,PAS]
```
specifies the `address` of the CD drive and the `interrupt`. The optional parameter `PAS` is for drives connected to Pro-Audio Spectrum sound cards.

Examples

```
cdu31a=0x340,5
```

specifies address `0x340` and forces interrupt 5

```
cdu31a=0x340,0
```

specifies address `0x340` and no interrupt

```
cdu31a=0x1f88,0,PAS
```

for connection to Pro-Audio Spectrum

Philips Laser-Magnetic Storage drive model CM-206

cm206=address,interrupt
> specifies the address of the CD drive and the interrupt.
> The address must be between 0x300 and 0x370, the
> interrupt between 3 and 11.

Examples

    cm206=0x340,5

specifies address 0x340 and forces interrupt 5

    cm206=auto

attempts to determine the address and the interrupt autonomously

Optics Storage 8000 AT CD-ROM

optcd=address
> specifies a certain address. 0 disables the driver.

Example

    optcd=0x340

Sanyo CDR-H94A CD-ROM (non-EIDE/ATAPI)

sjcd=address
> specifies a certain address

Example

    sjcd=0x340

Sony CDU-535/531 CD-ROM

sonycd535=address[,interrupt]
> specifies the address of the CD drive. Optionally, you can
> specify the interrupt.

Examples

    sonycd535=0x340

specifies address 0x340

73

```
sonycd535=0
```

suppresses probing

GoldStar R420 CD-ROM

```
gscd=address
```
specifies a certain `address`

Example

```
gscd=0x340
```

CD-ROM an ISP16 sound card

```
isp16=address[,interrupt[,DMA]],type
```
specifies the `address`. Optionally, you can specify the
`interrupt`, the DMA channel, and the `type`. The following
types are available:

`noisp16`	suppresses probing
`Sanyo`	for Sanyo CD-ROM
`Sony`	for Sony CD-ROM
`Panasonic`	for Panasonic CD-ROM
`Mitsumi`	for Mitsumi CD-ROM

PC loudspeaker   For loudspeaker support, you need to recompile
the kernel. Furthermore, a symbolic link must be set in the directory
`/dev`:

```
cd /dev
rm sound
ln -s pcsound sound
```

```
pcsp=rate
```
specifies a certain sampling `rate` in Hz. Specifying `off`
deactivates support.

Example

```
pcsp=8192
```

Sound cards   Sound card support requires recompilation of the
kernel. Furthermore, a symbolic link must be set in the directory
`/dev`:

```
cd /dev
rm sound
ln -s sbsound sound
```

The operation of sound cards is also described in the file `/usr/doc/howto/Sound-HOWTO.gz`. The boot parameter for sound card support takes the following form: `sound=0xTTAAAID`, whereby `TT` stands for the type of the sound card, `AAA` for the port address, `I` for the interrupt, and `D` for the DMA channel. The following sound card types are available:

01 FM Synth (YM3812, OPL3, Adlib)
02 SoundBlaster (1.0 to 2.0, Pro, 16)
03 Pro Audio Spectrum 16
04 Gravis UltraSound
05 Roland MPU-401 UART midi
06 SB16 (16 bit DMA number)
07 SB16 Midi (MPU-401 Emulation)

The interrupt is specified as a one-digit hexadecimal number (A to F for decimal 10 to 15).

Examples

```
sound=0x0222056
```

for a SoundBlaster at address `0x220`, interrupt 5, DMA channel 6

```
sound=0x13880
```

for AdLib sound cards

```
sound=0
```

disables sound support

Additional options   All boot options that have not already been listed are not interpreted by the kernel, but are passed to the `init` process. If the options contain an equals sign (`=`), they are set as environment variables. `init` passes the environment variables to the boot scripts. This makes it possible, e.g., to set a host name: `hostname=demo.sample.net`. Otherwise they are passed to

environment variable

75

init as command-line parameters. The options 0-9, s, or single
run level   allow you to set the run level.

7.2   The Linux Universe boot manager

The **Linux Universe** boot manager allows comfortable selection of
boot drive and   the drive and partition for booting. For Linux partitions, you can also
boot partition   select the boot options.

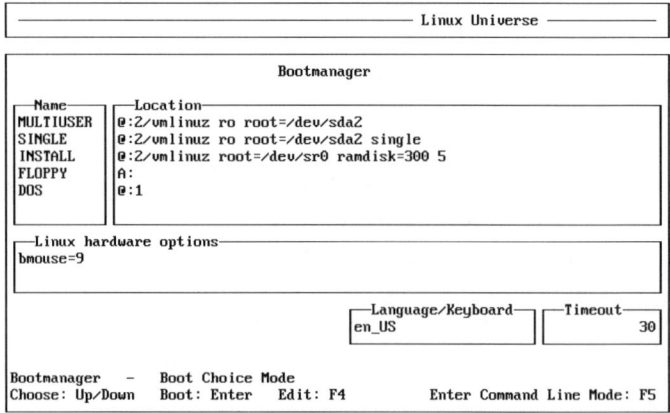

Figure 7.1. The boot manager

name   At the left is the name of the respective boot variant, which can
be selected freely. It is intended to help the user with orientation.
The field to the right thereof contains the boot drives and partitions,
whereby the Linux boot variants include the boot options. Under
options   **Linux hardware options** you have the options that more precisely
specify the hardware. They apply for all Linux boot variants. Under
language/keyboard you can select your type of keyboard. The
timeout   number entered under**timeout** specifies the number of seconds that
the boot manager waits for keyboard input before starting the default
boot variant.

Syntax of the boot configuration   The partition specifications
always have the syntax drive:partition. A or B indicate floppy

disk drives (since diskettes have no partitions, you specify none); C or D designate *physical* hard disks. The drive designation @ stands for the drive from which the boot manager was loaded. For the Linux boot configurations, right after the partition you must specify the kernel file; as a rule, this is /vmlinuz. Next you can specify other boot options, blank delimited.

partition and kernel

Note that the root file system is in principle independent of from where the kernel was loaded. For example, you could boot from diskette with

```
A:/vmlinuz root=/dev/sda2
```

and then work with the Linux hard-disk partition.

Examples

```
@:2/vmlinuz root=/dev/sda2 ro
```

This loads Linux from the second partition of a SCSI hard disk.

```
@:1
```

This entry suffices to load DOS from the first hard-disk partition.

```
A:
```

This entry allows booting from diskette.

Using the boot manager   The cursor keys allow you to select the desired boot configuration, which you then boot with (**Return**). (**F5**) gives you a command-line version of the boot manager, where help gives you an overview of available commands. menu returns you to the menu. The boot configuration that is to be activated automatically after the waiting time expires can be selected with the cursor keys and then set by pressing (**F3**). To change the individual fields, first press (**F4**) to enter editing mode. Then move the cursor with the cursor keys or with (**TAB**) to the respective field and press (**F4**) to activate it. After modifications, press (**F3**) to close the field again. Pressing (**F3**) again exits editing mode and activates your changes.

default

editing mode

As soon as you press one of the boot manager's function keys, the waiting time is suspended. This allows you sufficient time to make your changes.

7.3   Boot variants

active partition

If you operate DOS and Linux on one hard disk, it is easiest to mark the Linux partition as active with the `fdisk` command (of DOS or Linux). On booting, you then come to the **Linux Universe** boot manager, where you can set an option for your DOS partition. Alternatively, it is possible to boot DOS first and then to load Linux. If you install Linux on your second hard disk, this requires that you install the **Linux Universe** master boot record.

master boot record

Loading Linux from DOS   To be able to load Linux from DOS, observe the instructions on memory configuration on page 26.

Independently of whether Linux has been installed on a separate partition or in the directory `\LINUX` of the DOS partition, you can boot Linux from DOS.

In the former case, you can create the directory `\LINUX` on your DOS partition. Then copy the files `LOADLIN.EXE` and `vmlinuz` from the **Linux Universe** installation CD into this directory. Assuming that you have installed Linux on the second partition, for example, you can boot Linux with the following command:

```
loadlin vmlinuz root=/dev/hda2
```

The invocation for the Linux installation on the DOS partition is analogous, except that here, naturally, the DOS partition must be specified as `root` file system.

In both cases it is more comfortable if you put this boot command in a file `\LINUX\LINUX.BAT` and add the path `\LINUX` to the environment variable `PATH`. Then you only need to enter `linux` at the DOS prompt, and off you go.

menu definition

Alternatively, in your `CONFIG.SYS` file you can define a menu in which you can choose between DOS and Linux:

```
[Menu]

MENUITEM=DOS
MENUITEM=Linux
MENUCOLOR=15,1
```

```
MENUDEFAULT=Linux, 10

[DOS]

REM Instructions/driver for DOS

[Linux]

REM Instructions/driver for Linux
REM Example configuration:

BUFFERS=1,0
FILES=10
LASTDRIVE=Z
FCBS=1,0
DEVICEHIGH=C:\DOS\HIMEM.SYS
DEVICEHIGH=C:\DOS\EMM386.EXE
DOS=HIGH,UMB
STACKS=0,0

REM driver for controller and CD-ROM
```

Depending on your choice, in the section [Linux] of CONFIG.SYS you should eliminate all unnecessary drivers. Then if you insert the statement GOTO %CONFIG% at the proper position in your AUTOEXEC.BAT and in the section :Linux you include the command LOADLIN.EXE, then you can boot Linux from a menu:

```
GOTO %CONFIG%

:DOS
REM Instructions for DOS
GOTO End

:Linux
C:\LINUX\LOADLIN C:\LINUX\VMLINUZ
        root=/dev/sda2

:End
```

In this example we assume that the program LOADLIN and a copy of the kernel VMLINUZ are located in the directory \LINUX of the DOS partition. After booting, the second partition of the first SCSI hard disk is used as root file system.

If you have installed Linux on a separate partition, you can access the files on the DOS partition from under Linux as well. Here you need to create the directory /dos under Linux and then (assuming that DOS is on the first partition of the first SCSI hard disk) execute the following command:

```
mount -t msdos /dev/sda1 /dos
```

The corresponding command for the third partition of the second EIDE hard disk is:

```
mount -t msdos /dev/hdb3 /dos
```

You will find additional examples of the mount command in Chapter 8, "Fundamentals," and in the Reference.

The Linux Universe master boot record

The **Linux Universe** master boot record (MBR) allows you to select the drive and partition during booting. In particular, it is also possible

to boot from the second hard disk.

If you installed the **Linux Universe** master boot record with the installation program, this MBR responds on booting with a small menu:

```
C: X 1234 ABCD PQS ? _
```

Figure 7.2.   Linux Universe MBR

At the prompt you can enter [a], [b], [c], or [d] for the drive and the number of the desired boot partition ([1] to [4]) on the respective hard disk.

With [Enter] you continue the default booting procedure. If no default has been set, booting proceeds from the first partition that is marked active. This is automatic if you have not made an entry over a certain time. To vary the waiting time, press [q] (quicker) to halve or [s] (slower) to double the time. The minimum waiting time is one second.

The default that is automatically booted after the waiting time has elapsed can be set with (p) (preset). After you have pressed (p),   default you need to enter the number of the partition ((1) to (4)) or the drive letter ((a) to (d)). (?) disables the default and forces waiting for user input in every case.

If you want to boot from the second hard disk, you must install the **Linux Universe** master boot record on both hard disks. On booting, you enter (d). This loads the MBR of the second hard disk. Then you can initiate booting from the corresponding partition of the second hard disk with (1) to (4).

You can restore the DOS master boot record at any time under DOS with `fdisk /mbr`.

## Chapter 8

Fundamentals of Linux

8.1 First things first

Do not simply turn off the Linux system! First the command `shutdown` must be executed. This command is executed automatically when you initiate a reboot with [Ctrl] + [Alt] + [Del]. Failure to carry out a proper shutdown can cause inconsistencies in the file system because for disk access Linux uses buffers in RAM. These buffers must be written to the hard disk in a controlled way buffers before the system is turned off. To conduct a shutdown, log in as `root` and type in the command

```
shutdown
```

On display of the following message, you can turn off the computer:

```
Now you can turn off the power.
```

8.2 Accessing and removing the Linux Universe CD

Always execute the command `umount /dist` before you remove the **Linux Universe** CD from the drive; this informs the operating system that the CD is no longer available. The command

```
mount -t iso9660 -o ro /dev/sr0 /dist
```

makes your CD accessible again in a SCSI CD-ROM drive. Beginning on page 25 you will find a list of possible drives. To execute this command, you need to be logged in as `root`.

8.3   Accessing other file systems

The mount command (executed as root) also enables accessing DOS, OS/2, and Windows 95 partitions under Linux. Mount the directory tree of the respective partition onto a directory of the Linux directory structure. Assuming that a directory /import exists and the first partition of the first SCSI hard disk is to be accessed as a DOS partition, use the command:

```
mount -t msdos /dev/sda1 /import
```

Analogously, for an OS/2 partition use the command:

```
mount -t hpfs /dev/sda1 /import
```

For a Windows 95 partition use the command:

```
mount -t vfat /dev/sda1 /import
```

8.4   Linux identifiers

case sensitivity   Like all UNIX derivatives, Linux is case sensitive. This applies not only for the names of commands, files, and directories but also for users' login names and passwords. This means that the file names File1 and file1 are distinct and can coexist in the same directory.

Under the ext2 file system normally used with Linux, the names
maximum 255   of files and directories can be up to 255 characters long; the names
characters   can contain multiple periods (.) (e.g., report.Oct.1996) since Linux regards the period like any other character.

As in DOS, under Linux the wild card asterisk (*) allows specification of multiple files (e.g., for copying). The mask *.ps indicates all files that end in .ps, regardless of how many characters precede the ending. The mask * indicates every file, while *.* applies only to files whose names contain a period that is not at
hidden files   the beginning. Hidden files begin with a period and can be displayed with ls -la.

8.5   Users and groups

Every Linux user has a login name (e.g., the last name) and a password. The system prompts for both at the start of a session, whereby the password is not displayed as the user types it. The user's login name, actual name, and home directory are recorded in /etc/passwd, which also contains the group to which the user belongs, called the login group or default group. For security reasons, the encoded password is stored in a different file, /etc/shadow.

In addition to the default group, each user can be entered in additional groups in the file /etc/group. The command newgrp allows a user to change groups.

other groups

changing groups

A user's login name and group membership can be displayed with the command id. In addition to login and group names, this command displays the uniquely assigned number (called the ID). The assignment of IDs to the plain-text identifiers of the group and login names also occurs in /etc/passwd and /etc/group.

group membership

8.6   Files under Linux

Since Linux is a multiple-user system, each file has an owner and a group assignment. Normally the owner is the person who creates the file. In addition, each file has its own access rights, or permissions, which specify who can read the file, who has write privileges, and who may execute the file. These permissions are assigned for each of three classes of users: for the owner of the file, for the other members of the group to which the file is assigned, and for users outside this group. Finally, each file has a date that reflects its last modification.

user classes

8.7   Essential commands

This section provides an overview of everyday commands in UNIX. A complete description of available command options can be found in the Reference.

Changing the password

After a login, the password can be changed with the program
passwd. The program prompts first for the old password and then
twice for the new one (once for confirmation).

Directory listing

The contents of the current directory can be displayed with the
command ls. Optionally, a specific directory that is to be listed
can be specified. Thus ls Texts/ lists the contents of directory

verbose list   Texts. The command ls -l displays a verbose listing of each
file's information:

```
hera:/home/linux/lsdemo> ls -l
total 6932
-rw-r--r--   1 Eddy     users       41984 Sep 16  1995 HOWTO-mixwodka
lrwxrwxrwx   1 root     root           14 Jul  4 14:12 sample_link -> ../demo/target
drwxr-xr-x   2 linux    users        1024 Oct  4  1995 sample_subdir
-rw-r--r--   1 linux    users     3489714 Sep 16  1995 very.big.file
hera:/home/linux/lsdemo> █
```

Figure 8.1.   Example of directory contents

The first symbol indicates the type of directory entry: d means a
directory, l is a link, and b and c are block- and character-oriented
devices. The symbol - designates a regular file.

Next come the permissions for the file in groups of three
symbols, with the first three reflecting the rights of the owner, the next
three of other group members, and the last three of users outside the
group to which the file is assigned. In each of these three user classes,
r indicates read permission, w is write permission, and x shows
execute permission. After the permissions, you have the number of
references (hard links) to the file, followed by the owner, the file's
group, the file size in bytes, the date of last modification, and the file
name.

Changing directory

The current directory can be displayed with the command pwd.
Thecd command enables changing the current directory. cd ..
changes to the parent directory. cd - changes to the previous current
directory. Without parameters, the command changes to the user's

home directory. The home directory is always designated with a tilde   home directory
(~). Thus `cd ~/calc` changes to the directory `calc`, which is a
subdirectory of the home directory.

Creating and deleting directories

The command `mkdir` enables creating a directory. The command
`mkdir infos` creates the subdirectory `infos` in the current
directory. The command `rmdir` removes a directory, which must
be empty before deletion.

Changing permissions

The permissions on a file or directory can be changed with the `chmod`
command; this is defined in detail in the Reference. For directories,
observe that execute permission (`x`) has a different meaning than for   execute permission
regular files: it determines whether a certain user class can change to   for directory
this directory.

Copying, moving, and renaming files

The `cp` command copies files. `cp` always has two arguments, the
source file and the target file (in that order). If a file is to be copied
into the current directory, this must be specified explicitly with a
period (`.`). The command `cp *.txt Backup` copies all files that
end with `.txt` into the directory `Backup`, if it exists. Otherwise
the files are copied sequentially into a file named `Backup`. The
command `mcopy` enables copying from and to DOS diskettes. The   DOS diskette
command `mcopy a:'*' .` copies all files from the diskette in
drive A to the current directory. Note that in this case the asterisk
must be enclosed in single quotes; this is necessary for the correct
evaluation of the character. The `mv` command enables changing the
names of all files or directories or moving a file to another directory
(i.e., the file is copied and then the source file is deleted). As `cp`, `mv`
requires two parameters, the file to be moved and target name.

Changing owner and group

The group association of a file or directory can be changed with
the `chgrp` command. The owner of a file can be changed with the
`chown` command. `chown` also enables changing the group.

87

8.8   Redirection of input and output

You can redirect the output of a command with the > operator. The command ls > fileList writes the filenames of the current directory to the file fileList. The >> operator appends the output to an existing file. Analogously the input for a command can be redirected with <.

8.9   Piping commands

The pipe – operator enables the linking of commands; i.e., two commands are executed sequentially in such a way that the output of the first provides the input of the second. The command ps -aux – grep xteddy displays all xteddys that are currently running. xteddy is one of the most important programs under X11.

8.10   Accessing floppy disk drives

The easiest way to access DOS formatted diskettes is with the mtools.

➡ *Never use the* mtools *on a diskette that is simultaneously accessed with the* mount *command!*

To access diskettes with the Linux file system, you need to mount the corresponding device file in the Linux directory structure using the mount command. Assuming the existence of a directory /floppy for accessing the first floppy disk drive, the corresponding command for a diskette in the Linux Second Extended File System is:

```
mount -t ext2 /dev/fd0 /floppy
```

Thereafter the diskette can be treated like any other directory. The main directory of the diskette is in /floppy.

Important: *Before removing or changing a mounted diskette, execute the command* umount /floppy *to write the buffers to the diskette! The floppy disk drive must be remounted for each diskette!* Creating a diskette with Linux file systems is described in Chapter 9, Administration.

8.11   Virtual consoles

Under Linux you have up to eight virtual consoles available, with
the seventh being used by the X-Window system and the eighth
for standard error messages. Switch between consoles with **Ctrl** +
Alt + **F1** to **Ctrl** + **Alt** + **F8**.

8.12   Automatic path extension

The automatic path completion of the shell is quite useful. After you
input the first character of a file or directory name and press **Tab** ,
the shell tries to complete the name. If the starting letters do not
unambiguously match a name, the shell completes the name up to
the last unambiguous character.

completing file names

8.13   Compressed files

Compressed files end in .gz or .Z, depending on whether they were
created with gzip or compress. They can be decompressed with
gunzip or gzip -d, or with uncompress. The file extension
.tar.gz indicates that the file is an archive created with the
tar command and then compressed. Compressed tar archives
can be unpacked and decompressed at once with the command tar
-xvzf <file>.

8.14   Printing

Text, PostScript, and dvi files can be printed with the standard
installed filters using the lpr command. The lpq command lists
all printing jobs currently in the printer queue; lprm removes jobs
from the printer queue.

printer filters

8.15   Background commands

If you append the character & to a command, the command runs
in the background and you can immediately enter new commands
in the shell without waiting until a command has executed. This is

especially helpful under X11 when you invoke an application in an xterm. For example, you could launch emacs with the command emacs &, whereupon you can immediately enter further commands in xterm.

If such a command line is passed to the nohup command as a parameter, then the command continues to run even after the corresponding shell has been terminated by logout.

The shell's job control is also helpful. This allows halting a command while it is running and moving it to the background or foreground:

```
hera:/home/linux> emacs  Ctrl  +  z
Suspended
hera:/home/linux> jobs
[1]  + Suspended emacs
hera:/home/linux> bg 1
[1]  emacs &
hera:/home/linux>
```

In this example, first the emacs program is launched in the foreground. The key combination Ctrl + z halts this program, which the shell confirms with the message Suspended. Then the command jobs lists all processes that were started from the shell. Each process is preceded by a job number, by which the process can be moved to the background or foreground with the commands bg and fg.

8.16   Help and documentation

Invoke the online documentation (Manual Pages) for a given command with the man command. Thus man man provides the documentation of the man command. End the display of the documentation by inputting q .

documentation
of applications

The **Linux Universe** hypertext documentation, which is invoked with documentation, provides an overview of the software on the distribution CD and full-text searching by keyword. Descriptions of the individual software packages can be invoked there

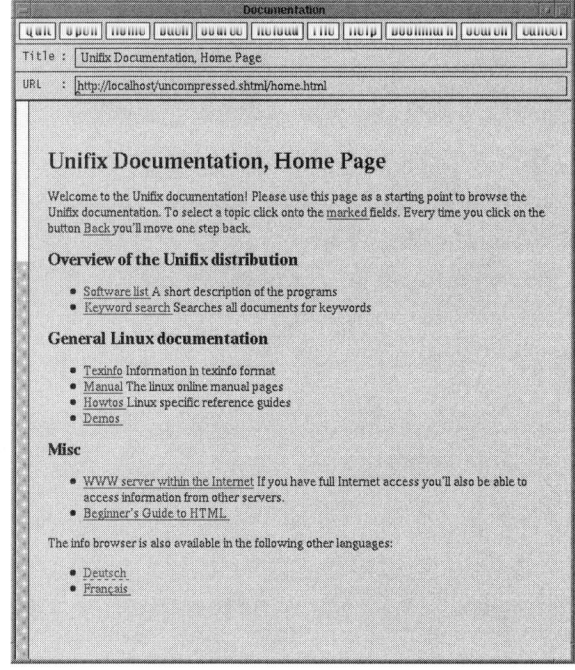

Figure 8.2. Hypertext documentation

as well as a subject-oriented overview of commands, demos, and the Linux HOWTOs.

The HOWTOs contain directions on subjects such as kernel compilation and operating various hardware components. All HOWTOs are in the directory `/usr/doc` (or as `.html` files in `/usr/html/howto`), which also contains other documentation. These files are packed in `.gz` format and so must be unpacked with `gunzip`. The files end with `.ps` after unpacking and can be viewed with `ghostview`, while those files with `.dvi` extensions can be viewed with `xdvi`. Both formats can even be printed on non-PostScript printers. Use the command `lpr` for printing. If necessary, you can convert `dvips` files from `dvi` to PostScript format. Furthermore, the directory `/usr/doc` contains the publications of the Linux Documentation Project:

HOWTO

91

- The Linux Installation Guide
    `install-guide.dvi.gz`
- The Users' Guide
    `user-guide.dvi.gz`
- The Network Administrators' Guide
    `net-adm-guide-1.0.dvi.gz`
- The Kernel Hackers' Guide
    `kernel_hackers_guide.dvi.gz`

Likewise under the **Help/Info** menu of the `Emacs` editor, you can view hypertext information on individual programs.

8.17   Fundamentals of X11

The most-used graphical user interface (GUI) under Unix is officially called `X Window system`, but it is also known as `X11` or informally as `X-Windows`.

Starting and ending X11

command-line invocation

Start `X11` from the command line with `startx`. End the GUI by simultaneously pressing [**Ctrl**] + [**Alt**] + [**Backspace**] or by clicking with the left mouse button on the free background. This raises a menu whose last option is **Exit**. If the program `xdm` is running, automatic log-out takes place.

Operating the X11 window

mouse emulation

The following description applies for 3-button mice. If you have a 2-button mouse, `X11` can simulate a 3-button mouse. Activate the entry `Emulate3Buttons` in the file `/etc/XF86Config`. Thereafter, pressing both mouse buttons simultaneously corresponds to pressing the middle button on a 3-button mouse.

The following is a standard `X11` window under the window manager `fvwm`. The window manager can be switched in the background menu.

Active window   All keyboard entries relate to the active window. By default, that window is active in which the mouse cursor is located. The active window is marked by its emphasized frame.

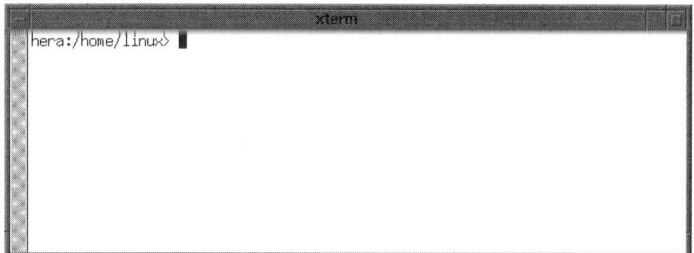

Figure 8.3. An X window

The window menu Open the window menu by clicking any mouse button on the symbol in the top left corner. Select the desired option with the left mouse button. Available options include **Delete** and **Kill**, with which applications in the active window can be deleted or terminated. Close the menu by clicking outside the menu window or with ⎡ESC⎤.

Iconizing Clicking with the left mouse button on the point in the top right corner closes the window and depicts the application as an icon at the lower edge of the screen. Double-clicking on the icon restores the window to its previous size.

Sizing Change the size of a window by shifting the left, bottom, or right edge using the left mouse button. Dragging the window corners allows changing the height and width simultaneously.

Clicking on the square in the top right corner toggles between the momentary window height and a preset maximized height. If the mouse button is kept pressed, the window expands to full screen height; double-clicking expands the window to the full screen size.

toggling window height

To change the size with the keyboard, press ⎡**Alt-F8**⎤, then use the cursor keys, and terminate with ⎡**Return**⎤.

Moving Move a window by putting the cursor on the window's title bar and then dragging the window with the left mouse button pressed. With the keyboard, press ⎡**Alt-F7**⎤, then use the cursor keys, and terminate with ⎡**Return**⎤.

Scrollbars Move the marker on the scrollbar with the middle mouse button pressed. If you press the middle mouse button on a

moving window
contents

position on the scrollbar, the mark jumps to the cursor position. With the left mouse button pressed, the mark moves down in small jumps; with the right mouse button pressed, it moves up.

Drawing a window into the foreground   Draw a window into the foreground by clicking the left mouse button on any position in the window frame.

Cut & paste

copying text

The cut & paste function allows copying text within a window or between windows. First mark the text to be copied by pressing the left mouse button; insert it at the target position using the middle mouse button. After marking, the left button can be used normally; the text remains stored until the next marking operation.

List of windows

Invoke a list of windows by moving the cursor to the background and holding down the middle mouse button. Releasing the button over a certain window entry activates the corresponding window.

## Chapter 9

Administration

9.1 What is administration?

The term *system administration* encompasses activities such as
registering new users, configuring hardware and the network,
compiling and configuring new software, and booting and shutting
down the system. All these activities are generally carried out by the
user root, also called the superuser, who has all permissions in the   superuser
system. However, this also means that root can create havoc. For
this reason you should only log in as root when this is explicitly
required. *Whenever you are carrying out activities that have nothing*   ←
to do with system administration, you should always log in as a
normal user! Then you can modify and delete only your own data.

9.2 xadmin

The purpose of xadmin

The program xadmin facilitates the configuration and management
of your **Linux Universe** system. xadmin allows you to carry out
numerous basic configuration and administration tasks with a mouse
under the graphical user interface X11 instead of with a conventional
text editor. The configurations of your file system, keyboard, and   graphical administration
much more are presented in an easily readable form. When adapting
your settings, you receive support from possible values and additional
information in the status line. Numerous settings can be made with   status line
the mouse alone. Modifications take effect only after you explicitly
confirm them.

You can exit any of the modules of xadmin at any time without
changing your system.

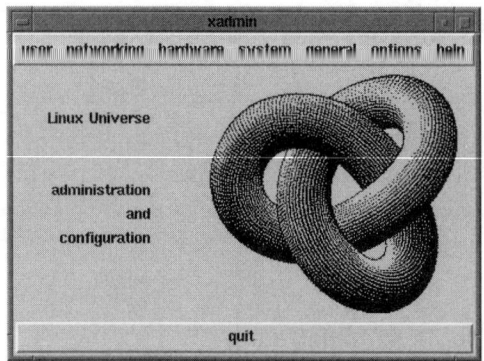

Figure 9.1. `xadmin`

As with many aspects of **Linux Universe**, including error messages and numerous Manual Pages, `xadmin` is bilingual. The language depends on the environment variable LANG. The contents of this variable consist of two parts: the first part is responsible for the language, and the second for country-specific aspects such as keyboard layout. Keyboard settings are made under `xadmin` in the module **keyboard** under **hardware**; the systemwide environment variables can be set in the module **environment variables** under **system**.

bilingual

If the first two characters of the environment variable LANG are de, then `xadmin` is German; otherwise it is English. However, you have probably already made your settings in the installation program.

General directions for using `xadmin`

When `xadmin` is launched, which only the user `root` can do, the program's top line displays a menu bar with the entries **user**, **networking**, **hardware**, **system**, **general**, **options**, and **help**. At the bottom of the window is the [**quit**] button, for terminating `xadmin`. Start the individual modules by clicking on a menu with the left mouse button and releasing the button over the desired menu item. Under **user**, e.g., you will find the modules **groups**, **shells**, and **users**.

modules

All modules have a status line at the bottom of the window. The information displayed there depends on the position of the mouse

status line

cursor; this includes the action that pressing a button would invoke and the meanings of the input fields.

Directly above the status line are usually the buttons **save & exit**, **cancel**, and **help**. The button **save & exit** leaves a module after saving the modifications. With **cancel** you can leave a module without consequences for the system. The button **help** displays the help text to the respective module in a separate window. The area above these buttons is module dependent, although the individual modules share a parallel structure.

cancel

Help system

Pressing the **help** button in any module or activating the menu item **usage** under **help** gives you the hypertext help system for `xadmin`. Each module has its own help text, and these texts are hyperlinked. The links are emphasized in the text, and clicking on a link with the left mouse button follows the link.

hypertext help

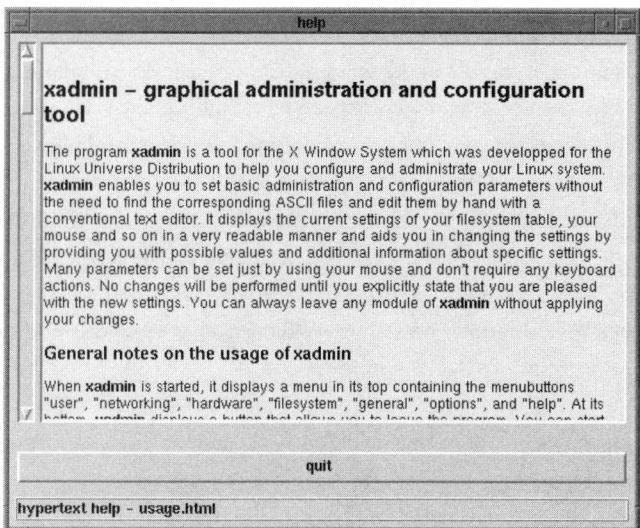

Figure 9.2. Help system

Color settings

The module **colors** in the menu **options** is for setting `xadmin` colors.

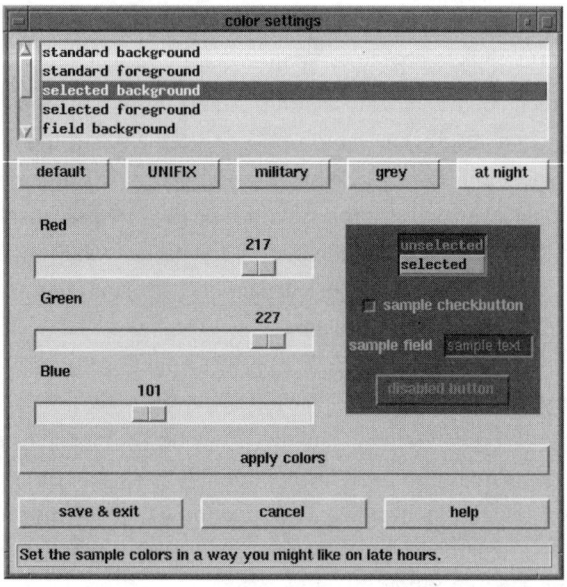

Figure 9.3. Color settings

change colors

example settings

The selection list in the upper area of the window contains a list of dialog elements whose colors can be set individually. If you select a color with the mouse, the corresponding red, green, and blue values of the slider are adjusted. If you shift one of the sliders, the change is reflected immediately in the example window to the right of the sliders. The buttons default, UNIFIX, military, grey, and at night provide example settings. If you are satisfied with the appearance of the example window, press the button apply colors to transfer the set colors to all xadmin windows.

Save the new color settings and simultaneously terminate the module **colors** by pressing the button save & exit. To exit the module without applying changes, press the button cancel; xadmin then restores the colors that you had before you invoked the module.

9.3 Software management

Linux Universe contains an extensive collection of important software packages that you can use in various ways according to

your personal preferences and needs. You can install all packages
that interest you or even the entire distribution (package all) on
your hard disk. In addition, you can use packages that are not yet on
your hard disk, but loaded from the CD (Live file system). Optionally,   Live file system
you can transfer files that you access in this way with the help of the
file cache, so that on further access the files are loaded directly from   file cache
the hard disk, which is faster.

The following sections explain how to install packages and how
to work with the Live file system and file cache.

In order to install packages and to work with the Live file system
and file cache, you must have mounted the **Linux Universe** CD to
/dist.

Package installation

For the installation and deletion of software packages, you can
choose between the xmsw under the graphical X11 and the
command-line-oriented programs swinstall, swremove, and
swlist.

Managing packages manually

swlist   swlist lists packages that are installed or contained in   listing packages
the distribution. For example, invoking swlist without parameters
displays a list of the installed packages, swlist @ /dist
provides a list of all packages contained in the distribution, and
swlist -v filecache outputs detailed information on the
package filecache. You will find additional information on
swlist in the corresponding Manual Page (man 8 swlist).

swinstall   You can install new software packages on the hard disk
with swinstall. Invoking swinstall graphics installs the   installing packages
software package graphics on the hard disk. swinstall has a
number of options; these are explained in the Manual Page (man 8
swinstall).

swremove   The counterpart to swinstall is swremove. The   deleting packages
name of the software package is passed as a parameter: e.g.,
swremove graphics deletes the package graphics from the
hard disk. The command swremove also has a Manual Page

(man 8 swremove), which explains additional options of lesser importance.

Package management with xmsw   Instead of using the command-line-oriented commands above, you can manage packages much more comfortably with xmsw under X11.

graphical management

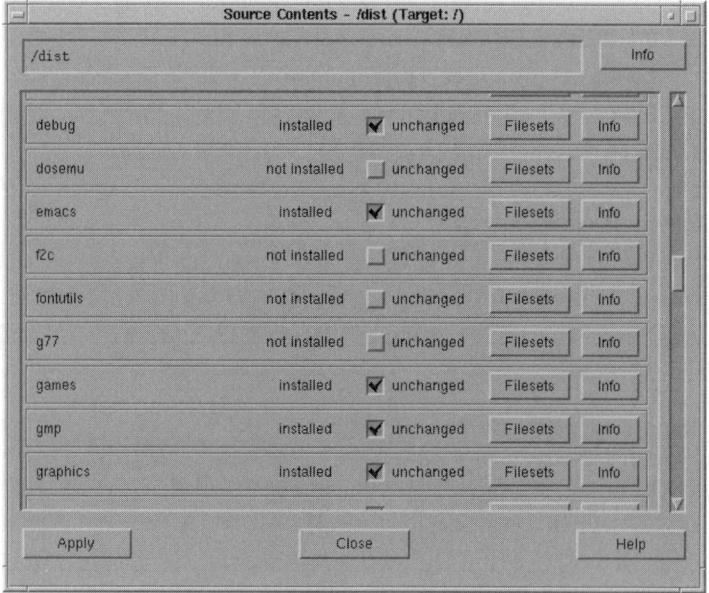

Figure 9.4.   Package management with xmsw

The program has detailed online documentation. xmsw allows mouse-driven installation and deletion of packages and subpackages, providing information on storage requirements along the way. Before a package is installed, the program tests whether the hard disk has sufficient space.

Live file system

To be able to directly execute files that are not on the hard disk, but only on the CD, the package cddep must be installed. For all files that are not installed, installing this package generates symbolic links

symbolic links

to the CD-ROM. Since the **Linux Universe** CD is in the directory tree under `/dist`, `/usr/bin/xteddy` would be a symbolic link to `/dist/usr/bin/xteddy`, as long as the program has not been copied onto the hard disk as part one of the packages `games` or by the file cache (see below) onto the hard disk and the symbolic link was thus replaced by the actual file. The drawback is that you have to put the CD-ROM into the drive to use these programs, and that programs load slower from CD-ROM than from disk. Also, if you uninstall software, links might be missing. In this case running `cddep on` restores all symbolic links.

The file cache

Purpose and function of the file cache   The file cache is a utility that temporarily stores files from slow file systems such as NFS or CD-ROM onto the faster hard disk medium. When a file is first accessed, it is copied onto the hard disk. When the space provided for the file cache is exhausted, older files without recent access are deleted to make room. This means that the initial access to a file is somewhat slower, while further access occurs at full hard-disk speed. In **Linux Universe** the file cache serves the purpose of *autocopy files* automatically copying files from the **Linux Universe** CD to the hard *to hard disk* disk to accelerate further access, although the file was not installed explicitly with the help of `xmsw` or `swinstall`. The advantage over a package installation is that exclusively those files are copied that are actually accessed.

   To allow the file cache to be active, in addition to the package `cddep` (see above), which creates and manages the symbolic links to the CD and thus the Live file system, you must install the package `filecache`. Furthermore, operating the file cache requires kernel support, which you should compile into the kernel if you intend to continue to use the file cache.

Configuration of the file cache   The configuration of the file cache is contained in the file `/etc/filecache.conf`. The most important entry here is `Max`, which allocates hard-disk space for the file cache, specified in megabytes (MB), kilobytes (KB), or *space allocation* percentage of the file system (%). If both an absolute size and a

101

percentage are specified, the smaller value applies. The entry Max 100 MB 50 %, for example, reserves 100 megabytes if the file system is at least 200 megabytes, otherwise 50 percent of the file system, for the file cache.

directory selection

The keyword Cache allows specification of the directories to be included, with both source and target directories. For example, the line Cache /dist/usr/man /usr/man includes the directory /usr/man in the file cache.

The file cache has other features. The corresponding Manual Page (man 8 filecache) provides details.

9.4 Configuration of the file systems

The components of the directory tree that is installed when your system boots are specified in the file /etc/fstab. Every line of this file corresponds to a file system. The first column of each line

devices

specifies the device name under /dev/; the second column specifies the path where the file system is to be mounted in the directory

type of file system

tree. The third column identifies the type of the file system. The most frequent types are ext2 for an Extended-2 file system, msdos for a DOS file system, and iso9660 for a CD-ROM file system. Also of importance are swap for a Linux swap partition, proc for the proc file system, which contains information on the state of the Linux system, and nfs for file systems mounted via the Network File System.

mount options

The fourth column contains comma-delimited options that are passed on mounting. These options are listed in the Reference to the command mount as well as in the corresponding Manual Page.

The fifth and sixth columns of the file /etc/fstab are of lesser importance. In the fifth column you specify how the respective file system is to be handled in dump commands in the creation of backups. For more information, we refer you to the literature on Unix system administration. For a normal Linux system you can safely enter 0 here. The last column is evaluated when checking the hard disks with the command fsck in order to ascertain the sequence of checks. The partition that is mounted to / should be checked first; here you specify 1. For the remaining hard-disk partitions, use 2. The

0 specifies that no check is necessary. This is the case, e.g., with CD-ROM file systems.

If you want to mount a DOS file system on the partition /dev/hda1 in the directory /dos as read only, insert the following line in the file /etc/fstab.

mounting DOS
file system

```
/dev/hda1 /dos msdos ro 0 0
```

Configuration of the file system under xadmin

The module **file system** under **system** enables setting the more common entries in the file /etc/fstab. Here you specify the devices or partitions that are to be mounted in the directory tree on booting. Enter them along with their path in the field **device**, e.g., /dev/hda1. The field **path** specifies where in the directory tree the respective device is to be mounted. It is common practice to mount an existing DOS file system in a directory such as /msdos. The column **file system** specifies the type of the file system, and in the column **mount options** you can specify the most important mount options (see the Manual Page on mount). These are ignored in the file system types proc and swap. (See Figure 9.5.)

proc, swap

The button **update** enters the settings for the middle window region in the list at the top edge of the window. The window contents correspond to the later appearance of the file /etc/fstab. The button **delete** removes the highlighted line from the list. Pressing **clear** deletes the fields **device** and **path**, activates an Extended-2 file system under **file system**, and sets the mount options to correspond to the option defaults.

The button **save & exit** stores the new settings in the file /etc/fstab, then terminates the module. To terminate the module without saving changes, use the button **cancel**.

9.5   Setting the keyboard type

The keyboard layout on the console and under X11 can be modified with the help of the command keyboard. Valid parameters are displayed by the command when it is invoked without parameters. The most common setting is en_US, for American keyboards.

keyboard command

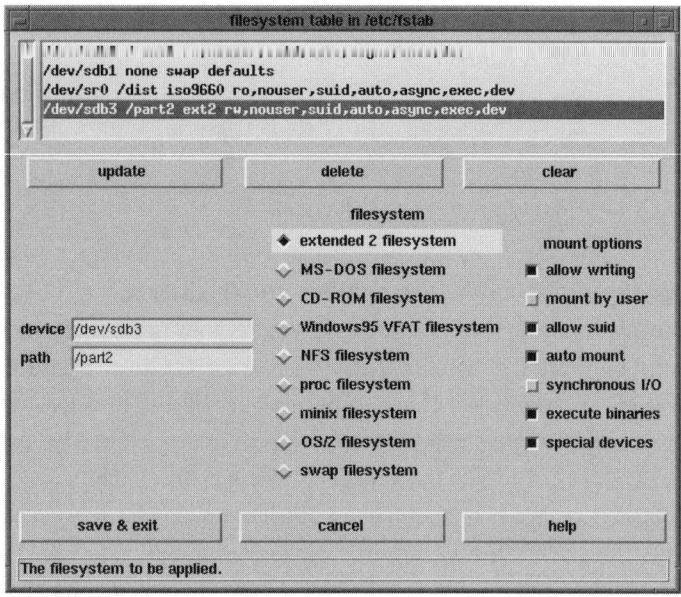

Figure 9.5. File system configuration

The settings are lost when you boot the next time unless you additionally enter them in the file /etc/KEYBOARD.

Setting the keyboard type with xadmin

Making keyboard settings is quite simple with the module **keyboard** under **hardware**. Select the appropriate keyboard type from the list and press **apply & exit** to save and activate the changes. This rewrites the file /etc/KEYBOARD, and the keyboard layout on the console and under X11 is reset. **cancel** lets you exit the module without any changes to the settings.

9.6   Processes

Because Linux is a multitasking system, you constantly have any number of processes running in parallel. Each of these processes is assigned a number, the process ID (PID). The command ps lists all running processes.

PID

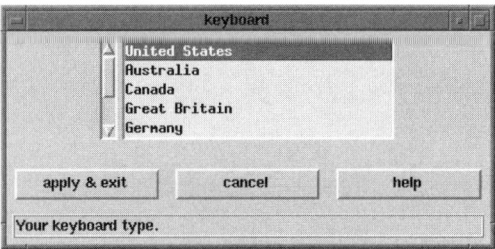

Figure 9.6. Keyboard settings

If a program fails to react to input and so cannot be terminated normally, its execution can be aborted with the help of the command `kill`. Here you need the process ID and optionally a signal (normally `15` for termination). The signal `KILL` has number `9` and is the most effective way to end a process. However, this signal does not leave the possibility of carrying out any concluding actions. Therefore, it should only be used if all methods have failed.

kill process

Example

```
$ ps | grep xteddy
5624 pp0 S 0:00 xteddy
5626 pp0 R 0:00 grep xteddy
$ kill -15 5624
```

Process management under `xadmin`

The `xadmin` module **processes** in the **general** menu helps the system administrator obtain an overview of running processes. It displays a list of the processes currently running on the system, sorted by process ID. For each process, the list indicates the user, the process ID, the percentage utilization of the CPU and the command line of the process. Under the process list there is an icon bar. The button update updates the process list; the buttons soft kill , hard kill , hup , usr1 , and usr2 send different kill signals to the selected process. After a signal is sent, the process list is updated. (See Figure 9.7.)

process list

CPU utilization

ending a process

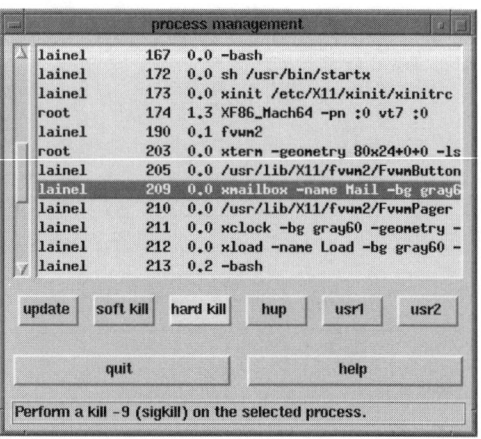

Figure 9.7. Process management

9.7 Shutting down the Linux system

cache, swap

Since Linux works with cache and swap mechanisms, there can be unpleasant consequences if a running Linux system is simply turned off. Furthermore, terminating processes in this way can also have harmful effects. In the best case the next booting takes longer because all hard-disk partitions must be checked.

halting the system

The command `shutdown` handles the proper shutdown of the Linux system. To shut down the machine, use `shutdown -h now`. This terminates all programs and brings the file systems into a consistent state. Then the system halts, and you can turn off your machine.

reboot

If you want the system to boot again immediately after a shutdown, use the command `shutdown -r now`. The same procedure is launched as with `shutdown -h now`; however, the system reboots the procedure at the end.

You can initiate a halt or a reboot of your system from `xadmin` with the modules **halt system** and **reboot system** under **general**. After a security check, a `shutdown -h now` or a `shutdown -r now`, respectively, is carried out.

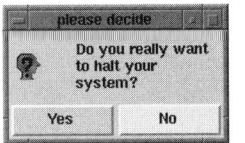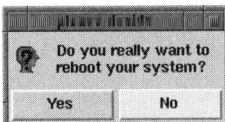

Figure 9.8. Halting and rebooting

9.8 Kernel modules

Kernel modules are object files that can be integrated into or removed from the Linux kernel at run time. This makes it possible, e.g., to add new drivers on demand without rebooting the system or recompiling the kernel. In the context of loadable modules, the commands depmod, modprobe, insmod, rmmod, lsmod, and ksyms are interesting. You will find more information in the corresponding Manual Pages.

changing the
running kernel

Likewise the file

```
/usr/src/linux/Documentation/modules.txt
```

proves interesting in this context. On booting, the boot files of **Linux Universe** attempt to integrate the kernel modules that are listed in the file /etc/MODULES into the kernel. With the xadmin module **modules** in the menu **system** you can add modules to or remove them from this file. The kernel modules to be integrated must be selected in the selection list.

The button **save & exit** writes the modifications to the file /etc/MODULES and exits the module. Modifications take effect only after the next boot. With **cancel** you can exit the module without applying the changes.

9.9 Utilities

Utility programs are usually daemons that run in the background and handle certain tasks. For example, the printer daemon lpd is a sort of print manager, the syslog daemon syslogd protocols important output and error messages of other programs (especially the daemons), the cron daemon serves the function of an appointment

daemons

lpd

syslogd

cron

calendar that starts processes at certain times, and the daemon `diald` automatically establishes connections to a terminal server when certain networks are accessed.

On booting, **Linux Universe** starts all utilities that are listed in the file `/etc/SERVICES`.

The `xadmin` module **services** in the menu **system** lets you select utility programs. Simply use the left mouse button to select the utility in the selection list to be started. If the settings match your wishes, you can store the changes in the file `/etc/SERVICES` with `apply & exit`, restart the utility, and exit the module. The button `cancel` exits the module without applying changes.

9.10   The appointment calendar `cron`

The daemon `cron` enables executing commands at certain times. If this has not been restricted by the system administrator, every user can create a sort of appointment calendar `crontab` (crontab), which is then checked minute by minute for tasks to be handled.

Thus, e.g., the system administrator can delete old log files, and users can automate their sending of birthday wishes. The prerequisite for a specified task to be handled by the cron daemon is, naturally, that the Linux system and `cron` are both running at the respective time.

automated birthdays

Configuring the crontab under `xadmin`

The `xadmin` module **crontab** in the menu **system** enables the system administrator to configure the cron daemon via the file `/etc/crontabs/root/crontab`. The module consists of two parts: In the first part, the environment variables for `cron` are set; in the second part, the appointment calendar itself can be edited.

Environment variables for `cron`   Initiate this part of the configuration of the cron daemon by pressing the `edit environment variables` button in the main window of the module. You will get a window that very much resembles that of the module **environment variables** and that enables setting environment variables which `cron` uses when it executes commands. The most common variables here are `SHELL`

SHELL, MAILTO

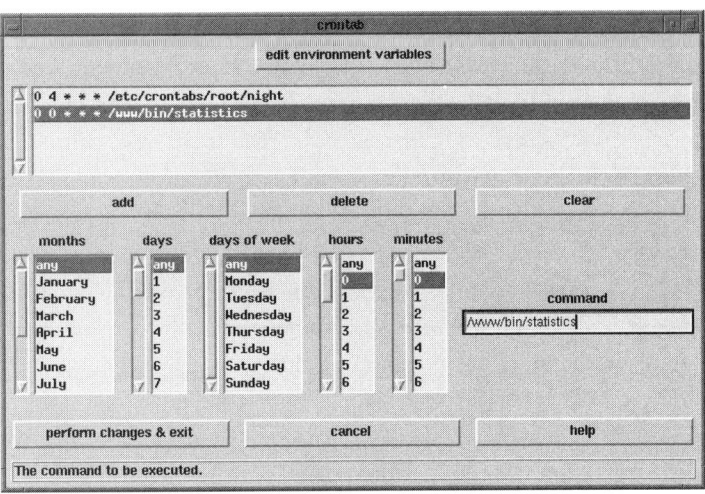

Figure 9.9. **crontab** management

(which shell should cron use) and MAILTO (user to whom messages should be sent).

To change the value of an environment variable, use the mouse to activate the corresponding line of the selection list. Then you can enter the field **variable's name**. With the button [update] you transfer changes to the selection list. To remove a variable from the list, activate the corresponding line and press the button [delete]. Add a new variable by pressing the button [clear], writing the name in the field **variable's name**, entering your value in the field **variable's value**, and finally pressing [update] to confirm the new variable.

With [save & exit] you confirm all changes and return to the main menu of the module **crontab**. The button [cancel] discards changes before exiting the window.

Editing the appointment calendar   In the selection list under the button [edit environment variables], the appointment calendar is represented as it is written to the file /etc/crontabs/root/ crontab after the button [perform changes & exit] is pressed. In the middle area of the window, you can edit individual lines of the appointment calendar, which always correspond to a cron job. In the column **months** you can activate the months in which the job is   setting times

109

executed, in the column **days** the days of the month, in the column **days of week** the weekdays, in the column **hours** the hours, and in the column **minutes** finally the minutes. The character * indicates

command   all possible values, e.g., all weekdays. The input field **command** specifies the command line that is to be executed at the specified time. If the command is to be supplied with input, this can be specified,

input   separated from the actual command by %, e.g.: echo %Hello! The button `add` is for adding the edited line to the selection list. `delete` removes the activated line from the selection list, and `clear` initializes the middle region of the window.

To write your changes in the appointment calendar to the file /etc/crontabs/root/crontab and make them effective, press the button `perform changes & exit`. With the button `cancel` you can exit the module without changing the configuration of the cron daemon.

Manually configuring crontabs

The commands for the cron daemon are first written in a special

crontab   format to a file of any name and then transferred to the cron daemon with the command crontab filename. Each line of the file corresponds to a task for cron. The first five columns of a line specify the times when a command line is to be executed; then comes the command line itself.

Complete information on the structure of crontabs is available

Manual Page   in the Manual Pages for the command in Sections 1 and 5, which are invoked with man 1 crontab or man 5 crontab.

9.11   User management

You can manage users quite comfortably with the xadmin module **users** under the menu item **user**.

Alternatively, you can create a new user with the command

useradd   useradd -m name and change a password with passwd name. If no home directory is to be created for the user, omit the -m.

userdel   Remove a user with the command userdel name. The parameter -r ensures that the corresponding home directory is also deleted.

User management with `xadmin`

The module **users** enables creating and deleting users. Furthermore, you can set user IDs, home directories, comments, passwords, shells, and groups for users quite simply.

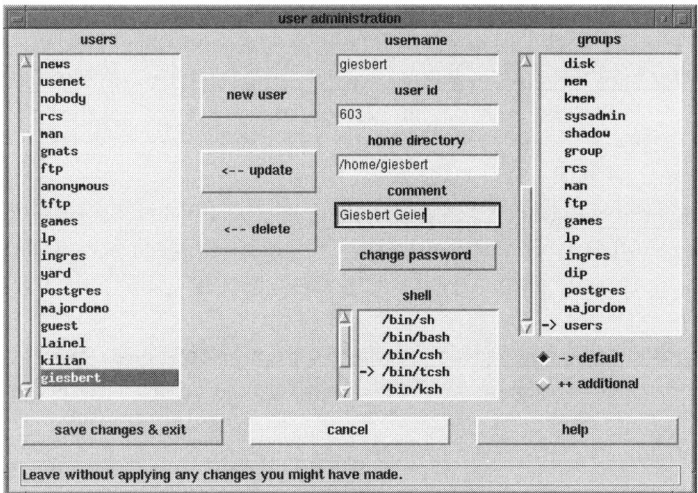

Figure 9.10. User management

The affected files are /etc/shadow, /etc/passwd, and /etc/group, though the first-named file may not be present. If the file /etc/shadow exists, then shadow passwords are supported, in which case the encoded passwords are not entered in /etc/passwd, but in /etc/shadow. Only root can read this file, which prevents users from copying the encoded passwords and decoding them with utility programs.

shadow passwords

Beyond the usual features at the bottom of the window, at the left the module contains a list of all users and at the right the settings that correspond to each respective user. In between are three buttons, **new user**, **update**, and **delete**. Whatever you do in the top area of the window, it takes effect only after you press the button **save changes & exit** at the bottom left.

user list

Adding a user   Press the button ⌊ new user ⌋. The next available user

user ID   ID is entered in the field **user id**. Likewise the shell and default group
(both configurable in the `xadmin` module **defaults**) have default
values. The other fields need to be entered. Enter the user name in the
field **username**. The field **home directory** receives an initial value
as soon as you edit the next field. Adapt this directory as needed,
and enter the comment for the new user, usually the full name. The
password is empty initially. Changing the password, shell, and group
affiliation is described below.

To enter the new user in the user list at the left, press the button
⌊ update ⌋.

Selecting a user   With the left mouse button, select a user from the
list at the left edge of the window. Then the corresponding settings
are displayed at the right side of the window and can be edited.

Changing a password   Press the button ⌊ change password ⌋. You
will obtain a small window with two input fields. All entered
characters are represented as asterisks (*) to prevent anyone from

enter password twice   reading them. To avoid typing errors, the password must be entered
in both fields. If you press ⌊ ok ⌋ and the entered passwords do
not coincide, you will receive a message and can make another
attempt. If the two entries do concur, the program remembers the
new password. The changes take effect after you press ⌊ update ⌋
to confirm the changes for the current user and finally the button
⌊ save changes & exit ⌋, which stores all changes made in this way.

Selecting a new shell   Click with the left mouse button on the shell
of your choice. In order to transfer the changes into the user list, you
must press ⌊ update ⌋. The list of possible shells can be configured with
the `xadmin` module **shells**.

Selecting the default and additional groups   To allow changing a

default group   user's default group, the button ⌊ –> default ⌋ under the group list must
be activated. By selecting a group with the left mouse button, you
can now reset the default group. Exactly one default group can be
selected; its ID is entered in the file `/etc/passwd` for the respective
user.

A user can also belong to additional groups. To activate or deactivate these with the left mouse button, the button **++ additional** under the group list must be activated. The additional groups are stored in the file /etc/group, which can also be edited with help of the xadmin module **groups**.

additional groups

In order to transfer the changes into the user list, you must again press the button **update**.

Deleting a user   Select the user as described above, and press the button **delete**. This removes the user from the user list at the left edge of the screen. The user is deleted permanently after you press the button **save changes & exit**.

Saving the changes   After you press the **save changes & exit** button, all changes that were transferred to the user list with the button **update** or **delete** are written to the corresponding files in the directory /etc/. Then the module terminates. With the button **cancel** you can quit user management at any time without changing the system.

For each new user, a home directory is created and files are copied to it from the directory /etc/skel/. In addition, the script /etc/xadmin/xadduser is executed with the parameters user name (username), user ID (userid), home directory (userhome), and shell (usershell). By adapting this script, you can carry out additional measures with the creation of each new user. Analogously, with each deletion of a user, the script /etc/xadmin/xdeluser is executed with the parameters user name (username), user ID (userid), and default group (usergroup).

Global settings for user management   The xadmin module **defaults** enables you to configure several settings that the module **users** employs. The parameter **default shell** indicates which shell is assigned to new users; **default group** defines to which group a new user is assigned; **default home** specifies where the home directory of a new user is created (do not forget to add the final character /).

default settings

9.12   User groups

All user groups that exist in the system are recorded in the file
/etc/group. Each line of this file is a four-column entry, where the
columns are separated by colons. The first column contains the name
of the group. The second column can optionally contain an encoded
group password   group password; however, group passwords are seldom used. The
third column gives the group ID; normally no two groups should
have the same ID. In the fourth column you have a comma-delimited
list of users for whom the group is an additional group (see user
management). You can specify the default group of a user via the
user's group ID in the fourth column of the file /etc/passwd.

Editing user groups with xadmin

You can edit the file /etc/group quite simply with help of the
xadmin module **groups** under **user**. The upper region of the window
displays the group list in the form in which it is maintained in the file
editing a group   /etc/group. To edit a group, select it with the left mouse button;
then you can edit the corresponding fields **group name** and **group
id**. All users for whom the selected group is an additional group are
selected in the list **group members**. Add or remove a user with the
left mouse button. (The default group for users is recorded in the file
/etc/passwd and can be edited with the module **users**.)

With the button update you can update the group in the list in
the upper region of the window or insert it there if it does not exist.
The button delete removes the selected group from the list. The
available group ID   button clear finds the first available group ID over 99 and enters it
in the field **group id** and clears the entries in the fields **group name**
and **group members**.

To apply your changes and to leave the module, press the button
 save & exit . With the button cancel you can exit the module without
applying changes.

9.13   Adding and removing shells with xadmin

A list of shells that can be assigned to a user is maintained in the file
/etc/shells. This is particularly relevant for the use of FTP, since

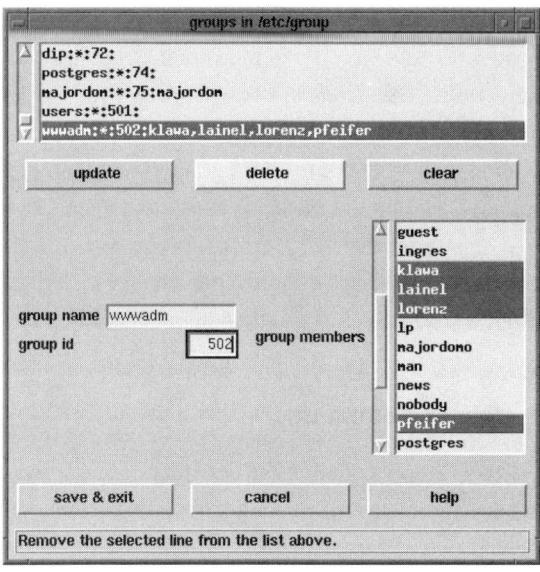

Figure 9.11. User groups

an FTP login checks whether the user shell entered in `etc/passwd` is recorded here as well.

The `xadmin` module **shells** under **user** handles the configuration of `/etc/shells`. This module displays the list of shells in the upper window region as this list is maintained in the file

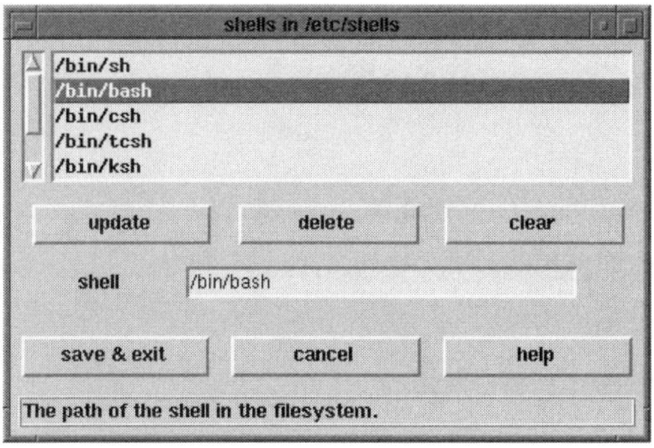

Figure 9.12. Managing shells

/etc/shells. All shells that are entered here and executable as well are listed for selection in the field **shell** of the module **users**.

• To remove a shell from the list, mark it with the left mouse button and press the button ⟨**delete**⟩. Add a shell by entering the corresponding path in the entry field of **shell** and then pressing the button ⟨**update**⟩. The button ⟨**clear**⟩ deletes the contents of this input field.

The button ⟨**save & exit**⟩ stores the changes, and the button ⟨**cancel**⟩ enables quitting the module without changing the system.

9.14   Message of the day

The file /etc/motd contains the text that is displayed on login. motd stands for message of the day. This provides a simple way to pass information to the users of the system.

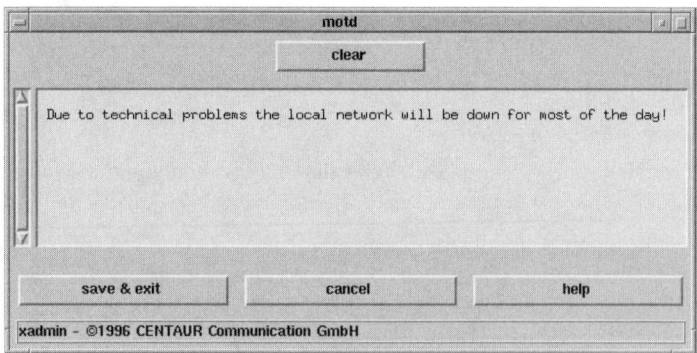

Figure 9.13. Message of the day

This text can be edited in any text editor or with the xadmin module **motd** under **general**.

9.15   Boot message

login prompt   The file /etc/issue is displayed on the console before the login prompt. As with the file /etc/motd, you can edit it with the `xadmin` module **issue** under **general** or with any text editor. (See Figure 9.14.)

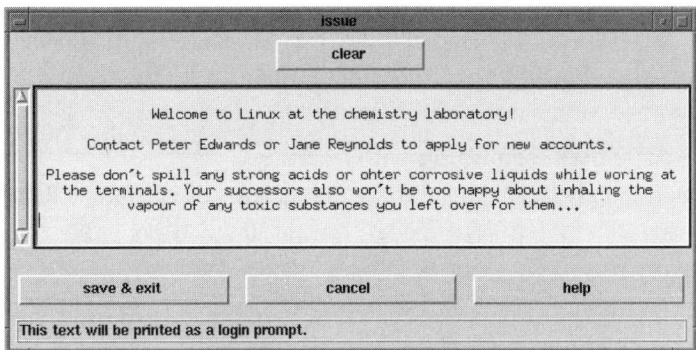

Figure 9.14. Login prompt

9.16 Formatting floppy disks

Low-level formatting

Low-level formatting of floppy disks under Linux is done with the command `fdformat`. Specify the appropriate device file as parameter. You will find a list of these files in the Manual Page for `fdformat`. If you pass the parameter `-n` before the device file, there is no check of the floppy disk. If you are accustomed to using an operating system like DOS, you will be pleased at how little the Linux system pays notice to the formatting process: while a floppy disk is being formatted, you can continue other work without restriction.

fdformat

check

Installing an Extended-2 file system

The command for installing an Extended-2 file system on a hard disk or floppy disk is `mke2fs`. As argument, specify the device file (`/dev/fd0` for the first, `/dev/fd1` for the second floppy disk drive). Before the device, you can pass a number of parameters. The most practical invocations for formatting a floppy disk are probably `mke2fs -m0 device` (no check) and `mke2fs -c -m0 device` (with check).

mke2fs

Installing a DOS file system

mformat

You can also install a DOS file system easily on a low-level formatted floppy disk with the command mformat, an mtools component. As under DOS, supply the argument a: for the first or b: for the second floppy disk drive. You can also specify the number of tracks (-t number), heads (-h number), and sectors (-s number)

floppy disk label

as well as the label (-l label) for the floppy disk.

Floppy disk formatting with xadmin

More simply than with the above commands, you can format floppy disks with the xadmin module **format floppy disks** in the menu **hardware**.

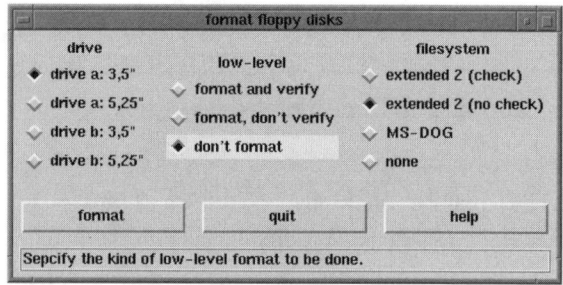

Figure 9.15. Formatting floppy disks

In the column **drive** you can select the floppy disk drive; in the column **low-level** you specify whether the floppy disk is to be low-level formatted with subsequent check, without check, or not at all. In

selecting the file system

the column **file system** you decide among an Extended-2 file system with or without check, a DOS file system, or no file system at all. The latter suffices, e.g., for creating a tar archive on floppy disk.

start formatting

The button [**format**] starts formatting. If there are problems, an appropriate message is displayed; otherwise there is a message after successful formatting of the floppy disk. The button [**quit**] terminates the module.

9.17   Copying floppy disks

Linux offers numerous ways to copy a floppy disk. Extended-2 floppy
disks can be mounted in the directory tree with the command `mount`   mount
and then can be read and written normally. This is also possible with
DOS floppy disks, although here accessing via the `mtools` proves   mtools
simpler, especially if you are accustomed to DOS. *When working*
with a mounted floppy disk, it is easy to forget to unmount the floppy
disk from the directory tree with `umount` *before removing it from*
the drive. This can cause errors and can have negative consequences
for the contents of the next floppy disk put in the drive, because data
might be written to it that were intended for the previous floppy.

Copying floppy disks with `xadmin`

It is very easy to copy an entire floppy disk with the `xadmin` module   copying a
copy floppy disks in the menu **hardware**. Regardless of the file   whole diskette
system, the entire floppy disk in the selected drive is copied using
the command `dd`, which is described in detail in the Reference.

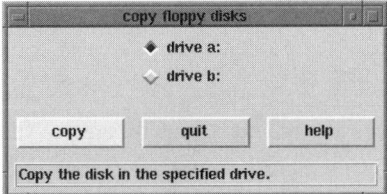

Figure 9.16.   Copying floppy disks

Select the correct floppy disk drive and press **copy** to start
copying. You will be prompted to insert the source diskette. After
the source has been read completely, you will be prompted for
the target, which is then written with the contents of the source
diskette. Messages indicate problems or successful completion. Exit
the module with the button **quit** .

9.18 Setting date and time

date, clock   The system time can be set under Linux with the commands date and clock. This is simpler with the xadmin module **date & time** under **general**.

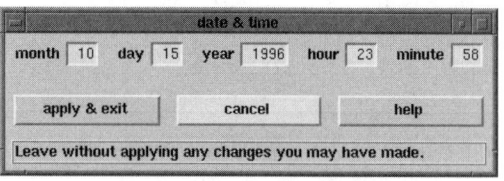

Figure 9.17.   Date and time

This module enables you to set your system time. Five input fields display the system time when the module is started. These can be edited to set the correct time. Simply enter the corresponding values in the fields **month**, **day**, **year**, **hour**, and **minute**.

When you press the button apply & exit , you set the specified time as the system time and terminate the module. The button cancel lets you exit the module without changing the system time.

9.19 Backups

Anyone who uses a computer seriously creates files that must not be lost, even if something goes wrong. *Linux has no* undelete *command!* All too quickly you might enter rm * old instead of rm *old (and thus delete not the files ending with old, but all files). To avoid helpless depression at such a time, the most important files need to be backed up regularly.

streamer   The best device for such a backup is naturally a streamer (especially a DAT streamer), but due to their price they are seldom found in personal hardware configurations. Fortunately, the GNU version of the command tar, which is most often used for backups, also supports archives that extend over multiple floppy disks. backups on floppy disk   This enables backing up even relatively large quantities of data comfortably on floppy disk.

Backup on streamer

Linux supports three types of streamers:

- SCSI streamer
- QIC-80 and compatible streamers attached to a floppy controller
- IDE ATAPI streamer

All streamers share common usage with `tar`. The name of the device that is specified with the `tar` command depends on the streamer you use. For simplicity's sake, however, you can create a link `/dev/tape` that references the corresponding device; then you can access the streamer via `/dev/tape`. The first SCSI streamer (with automatic rewind) would use the following commands:

```
# rm /dev/tape
# ln -s /dev/rst0 /dev/tape
```

The following sections describe the device names of the individual streamer types. To back up the directory `/home/fred`, enter the following command:

```
tar cvf /dev/tape /home/fred
```

The following command completely restores the contents of a streamer tape to the hard disk:

```
tar xvf /dev/tape
```

SCSI streamer For the kernel to support a SCSI streamer, the corresponding driver must either be available as a module or compiled into the kernel (option `SCSI tape support`). By default the driver is a module (`/lib/modules/2.0.XX/scsi/st.o`) that is loaded automatically whenever the corresponding device file is accessed. If necessary, the module can be loaded or removed with the command `insmod` or `rmmod`, respectively.

Alternatively, the first streamer with automatic rewind can be accessed via `/dev/st0` or `/dev/rst0`. The device names for the no-rewind variants `/dev/nst0` or `/dev/nrst0` are analogous. For the second streamer, specify `/dev/xxst1` analogously.

121

The program `mt` enables one to rewind a tape:

```
hera:/home/mdorf> tar cvf /dev/nrst0 demos/
hera:/home/mdorf> mt -f /dev/nrst0 rewind
```

block size In addition, you can set the streamer's block size with `mt`. This might be necessary if you are exchanging tapes between two DAT streamers that have different block sizes via BIOS settings. The following command sets a variable block size:

```
mt -f /dev/st0 setblk 0
```

More information can be found in the Manual Page for `mt`. The operation of SCSI streamers is also described in

```
/usr/doc/README.tape.gz.
```

Floppy streamer The driver for floppy streamers is by default also a module that is automatically loaded into the kernel when the device is accessed; this module `ftape.o` is located under `/lib/modules/2.0.XX/misc`.

The first floppy streamer with automatic rewind can alternatively be accessed via `/dev/ftape` or `/dev/rft0`. The corresponding device name for the no-rewind variant is `/dev/nftape` or `/dev/nrft0`. For the second streamer specify `/dev/xxft1` analogously.

Find additional instructions for operating floppy streamers in the file `/usr/doc/howto/Ftape-HOWTO.gz`. Thus far it is not possible to format floppy tapes under Linux. This requires formatting under DOS first or using preformatted tapes. Before using them, you must erase preformatted tapes:

```
mt -f /dev/ftape erase
```

IDE ATAPI streamer To support IDE ATAPI streamers, the kernel must be recompiled with the option `Include IDE/ATAPI tape support`. The first streamer is accessed via the device `/dev/ht0` (rewind) or `/dev/nht0` (no rewind).

Backup on floppy disk

For floppy disks that you intend to use for `tar`, you need not install a file system; they only need to be low-level formatted. When backing up on floppy disks, avoid compressing the files; in the event of a disk error you can lose everything. With the following command you generate a `tar` archive on floppy disks that contains the directory `v-name`:

```
tar -Mcvf /dev/fd0 v-name
```

When one floppy disk is full, you are prompted to insert the next. Unpack the archive again by inserting the first diskette and entering:

```
tar -Mxvf /dev/fd0.
```

You can display the directory of an archive with `tar -Mtvf` `/dev/fd0`. The option M stands for multivolume, and `/dev/fd0` is the device of the first floppy disk drive; the second is `/dev/fd1`. A detailed description of the `tar` command can be found in the Reference.

9.20   Environment variables

Environment variables enable storing information that programs can employ. The environment variable `HOME`, e.g., contains the user's home directory, where many programs save their configuration files.

home directory

With the command `printenv` you can output all current environment variables and their values.

Environment variables are created differently depending on the shell used. The variable `DISPLAY`, e.g., where X-clients read the X-server to be used, is created and set in a `bash` with `export` `DISPLAY=zeus:0.0` and in a `tcsh` with `setenv DISPLAY` `zeus:0.0`.

Systemwide environment variables

In the file `/etc/ENVIRONMENT` **Linux Universe** systems contain a list of environment variables that apply for all users. Changes to this file take effect only after a reboot.

The module **environment variables** lets you edit this file. The list at the top of the window contains the variables and their values. Mark a variable in the list with the left mouse button. Then enter or

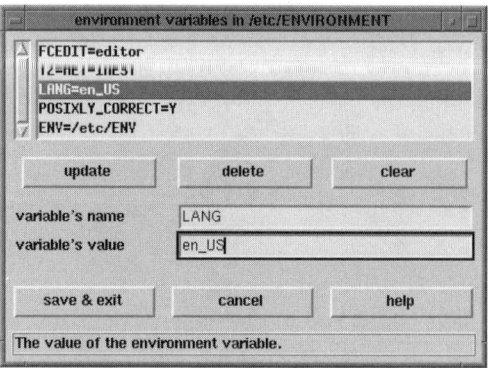

Figure 9.18. Environment variables

edit the variable name and the corresponding value in the respective fields in the middle area of the window. The button **update** transfers the entries to the list. Remove the marked line from the list with the button **delete**. **clear** clears the input fields **variable's name** and **variable's value**.

9.21 Printer configuration

Setting the printer port

parallel port

The xadmin module **printer port** under **hardware** enables you to set the parallel port of your printer. As a rule /dev/lp1 corresponds to the first port and /dev/lp2 to the second. In exceptional cases, /dev/lp0 can be the first parallel port.

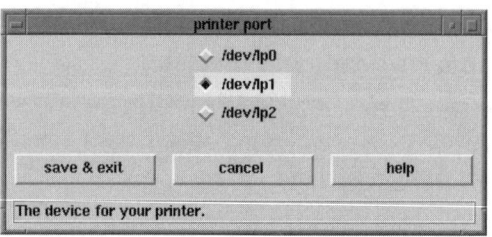

Figure 9.19. Printer port

The setting is realized via the symbolic link /dev/printer   symbolic link
to the selected device file.

Select the appropriate port and press **save & exit** to apply the
change. The button **cancel** exits the module without changes.

Printer configuration

The xadmin module **printer** under **hardware** supports printer
configuration via the file /etc/printcap. Select from the list
your printer or one that is similar. Then select the corresponding line
with the mouse and press **save & exit**.

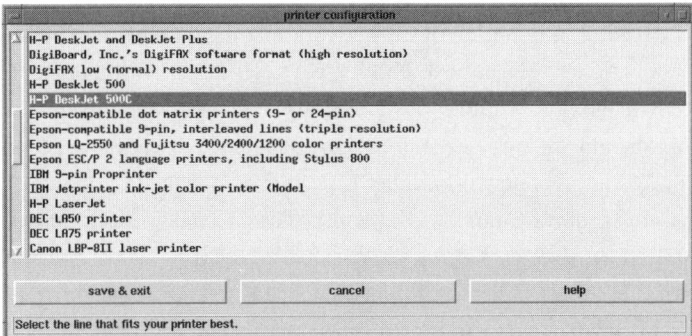

Figure 9.20. Printer configuration

If none of the settings proves successful, then certainly
studying the printing HOWTO (/usr/doc/howto/Printing-   printer HOWTO
HOWTO.gz, unpacked with gzip -d or gunzip) will help you.
However, be patient, for there are reasons why this file is so long.

9.22   Setting the modem port

The xadmin module **modem** under **hardware** enables you to
configure your modem serial port. Select the appropriate port and   serial port
press **save & exit** to apply a change. The button **cancel** exits the
module without changes.

The setting is realized via the symbolic link /dev/modem to
one of the device files /dev/cua0 to /dev/cua3.

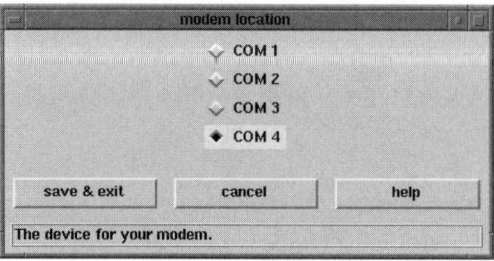

Figure 9.21. Modem configuration

9.23   Network

The basic configuration of the network in a **Linux Universe** system
with `xadmin` is almost child's play. However, a fundamental
knowledge of TCP/IP is necessary and is not covered in
this handbook. An excellent and detailed presentation of the
configuration of networks under Linux appears in the *Linux Network
Administrator's Guide* by Olaf Kirch. This is available as a `dvi` file
under `/usr/doc/net-adm-guide-1.0.dvi.gz` or as a book
from O'Reilly publishers. If you do not need to know everything, but
simply want to gain a quick overview, the current edition of the book
Linux: Unleashing the Workstation in Your PC by Stefan Strobel and
Volker Elling provides a good introduction to all network aspects
under Linux.

TCP/IP-configuration under `xadmin`

The `xadmin` module **tcpip** in the menu **networking** enables you to
network parameters   set the network parameters **hostname**, **NIS domain**, **name server**,
news server, **order** (for searching for IP addresses), **IP address**,
netmask, **broadcast**, and **gateway**.

All these values are also combined in the file `/etc/NETCONF`,
which is employed by **Linux Universe** boot scripts.

To change the settings, edit the corresponding input fields in the
`xadmin` module **tcpip**.

For the fields **NIS domain**, **netmask**, **broadcast**, and **gateway**
the module suggests values as soon as the field **hostname** or **IP
address** is entered.

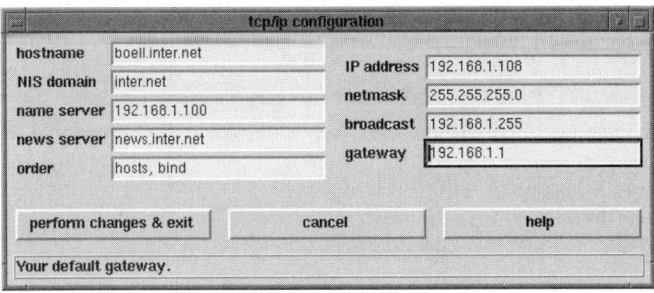

Figure 9.22. Network configuration

The button **perform changes & exit** saves and activates the new parameters and exits the module. Exiting the module by pressing the button **cancel** discards changes.

Directory of host names
The file `/etc/hosts` contains a list of IP addresses with corresponding host names and, optionally, other aliases for a host. The `xadmin` module **hosts** in the menu **networking** enables editing this list under `xadmin`.

IP address

alias

To add a host, press **clear** to clear the fields **IP address**, **hostname**, and **aliases** so that you can enter the data for the new

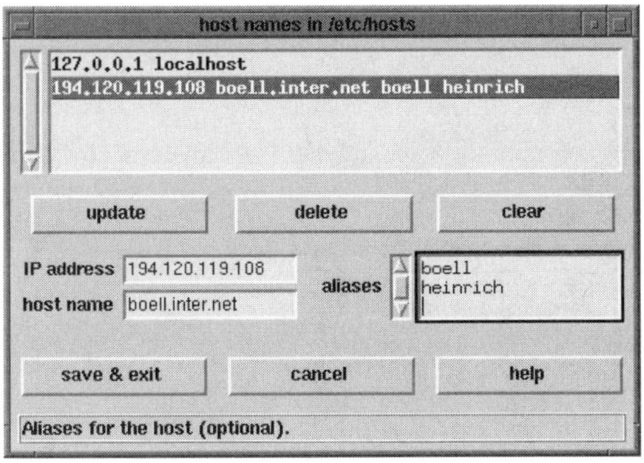

Figure 9.23. Host names

127

host; press **update** to transfer the data to the list. The button **delete** removes the marked line from the list.

Depart from the module with **save & exit** to write the file /etc/hosts or without changes by pressing the button **cancel**.

The file /etc/hosts.equiv

The file /etc/hosts.equiv contains a list of hosts that are viewed as equivalent. This means, e.g., that a user who has the same user ID on the two hosts can log in to this user's account on the host with the corresponding entry without providing a password in

rlogin rlogin. In addition to a host, each entry can contain a user name. This gives the respective user all permissions on the corresponding host host1 via the etc/hosts.equiv file; in particular, this user can log in as root via rlogin -l root host1 without a password.

Editing /etc/hosts.equiv **under** xadmin The xadmin module **equivalent hosts** under **networking** displays a list at the top of the window with information from the file /etc/hosts.equiv. The middle region allows you to edit a line. The button **add** appends the edited line to the list, **delete** removes the marked line from the list, and **clear** deletes the entries **address** and **user** of the edited line.

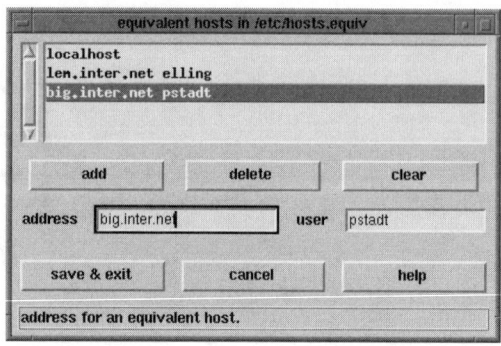

Figure 9.24. Equivalent hosts

When you press the button ⟨ **save & exit** ⟩, the information from the list is written to the file /etc/hosts.equiv and the module terminates. ⟨ **cancel** ⟩ quits without file modification.

The file /etc/hosts.lpd

The printer daemon lpd checks the file /etc/hosts.lpd in addition to /etc/hosts.equiv when an outside host seeks to place a print job in the printer queue. If a host only needs permission to print, then for security reasons it should only be entered in /etc/hosts.lpd. As with /etc/hosts.equiv, here the host name can be restricted with a user name.

print permission

Editing /etc/hosts.lpd **under** xadmin The operation of the corresponding xadmin module **printing hosts** in the menu **networking** corresponds to that of the module **equivalent hosts** (see above).

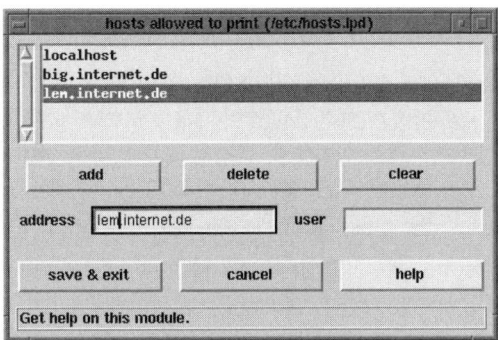

Figure 9.25. Printing hosts

NFS exports

The xadmin module **NFS** is for editing the file /etc/exports.

Here you can configure which directories of your own host (in its role as NFS server) other hosts (the NFS clients) can mount via NFS. The file is read by the NFS mount daemon rpc.mountd and by the NFS file server daemon rpc.nfsd. (These two are combined in the xadmin module **services** under the designation NFS daemon.)

NFS server
NFS client

129

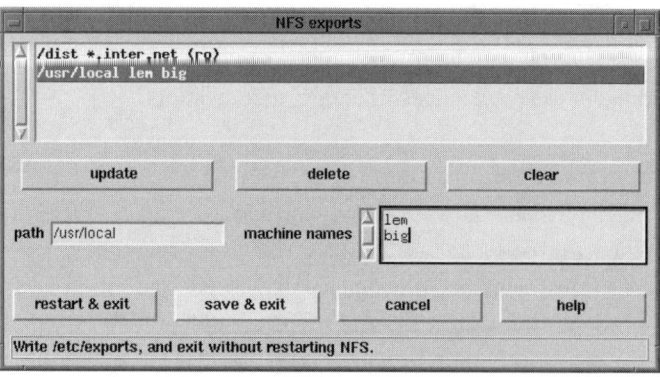

Figure 9.26. NFS configuration

The list in the upper window region contains the information from the file /etc/exports. To edit a line, click on it with the left mouse button. The corresponding information is then displayed in the middle window region. The field **path** contains the path in the local file system to be exported. The field **machine names** contains

options   a line for each client where the client is defined with any options in parentheses; the most common entry is the option (ro), which indicates that the directory can only be read by the client, who has no write permission. Other options are described in the Manual Page

host address   for exports. The host address can be specified symbolically or as an IP address.

To transfer the information to the list, press the button **update**. The button **delete** removes a marked line from the list, and the button **clear** clears the fields **path** and **machine names**. There are two ways to write changes to the file /etc/exports. **restart & exit** quits the module after the file has been written and the daemons rpc.mountd and rpc.nfsd have been restarted. This immediately activates the changes. The button **save & exit** does not restart the daemons. With **cancel** you can quit the module without rewriting /etc/exports.

Internet Access

Linux Universe provides easy Internet access via SLIP or PPP. Make sure that you have loaded the kernel modules `ppp` and `slip`. To set up the modem link automatically on demand, you must start `diald`. This should be enabled in the file `/etc/SERVICES` by adding:

```
# starting diald
/etc/diald/diald.run
```

This can be also done with `xadmin`. `diald` sets up a modem connection on demand if any program sends out an IP packet over the serial interface. It interrupts the connection after several minutes if there is no IP traffic. Terminate the connection by killing the daemon manually (or within `xadmin`):

```
root:>killall diald
```

For further information on `diald`, see the corresponding Manual Page.

To set up a PPP connection, you have to know several parameters. Your Internet provider should be able to tell you the necessary options. (See Figure 9.27.)

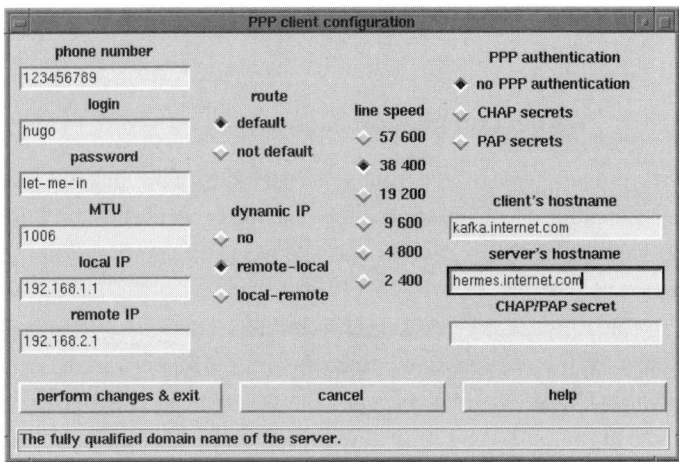

Figure 9.27. PPP configuration

If you prefer a SLIP connection, complete the appropriate dialog. (See Figure 9.28.)

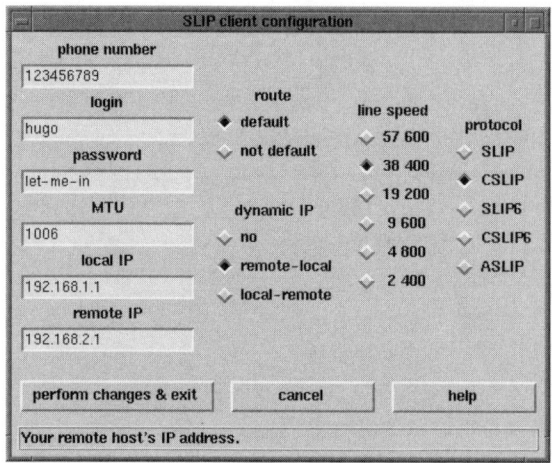

Figure 9.28. SLIP configuration

In special cases it might be necessary to edit the login chat script. (See Figure 9.29.)

After changing any of the SLIP or PPP parameters, restart `diald` by clicking the **perform changes & exit** button.

9.24   Kernel compilation

kernel tasks   The primary task of the Linux kernel is memory management and allocation of processor time to running processes. In addition, the kernel constitutes the interface between the hardware and the processes.

The **Linux Universe** kernel is initially configured to support as many systems as possible. Since the drivers for network adapters and most CD-ROM drives are available as kernel modules that can be linked at run time, the **Linux Universe** kernel since Version 2.0.x is no longer as bloated as in previous versions. Nevertheless, you can improve performance with a recompilation that is adapted to your

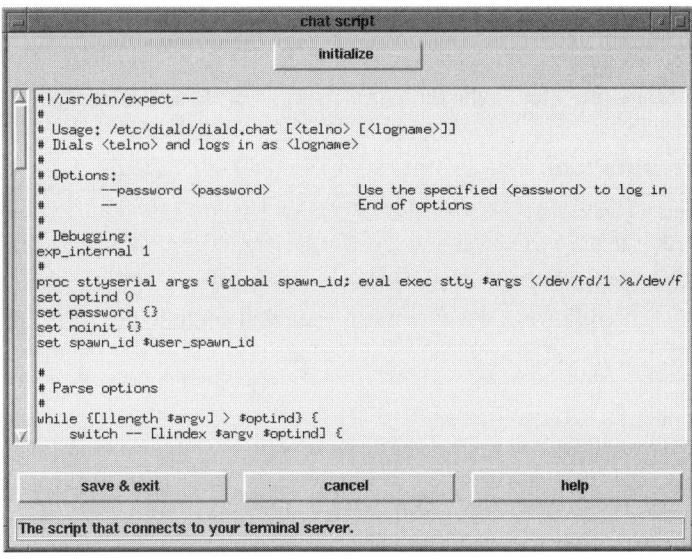

Figure 9.29. Chat script

system, significant features of the kernel can be defined individually, and important drivers can be hard-linked.

Recompiling the Linux kernel might seem quite ominous; indeed this is really the core (hence kernel) of your Linux system. On the other hand, this is the particular attraction of recompilation. What other operating system affords you the chance to cast a look into the source code and to adapt it to your needs by recompilation?

Actually, you are taking no real risk in compilation because the old kernel is retained and can be reactivated if needed. Furthermore, configuration and compilation certainly pose no insurmountable hurdle.

no risk to compilation

Modules

Loadable kernel modules provide one way to keep the kernel lean. Drivers that are available as modules need not be compiled into the kernel, but can be loaded and removed at run time with the commands `modprobe`, `depmod`, `lsmod`, `ksyms`, `rmmod`, and `insmod`. Loadable kernel modules exist to support parallel printers (`lp`), SLIP (`slip`), and PPP (`ppp`). Meanwhile most file systems,

dynamic driver

133

CD-ROM drives, and network adapters are supported in this way. You need not compile the kernel modules for kernel Version 2.0.18; they are provided in the directory /lib/modules/2.0.18.

Preparations

In the following we assume that you intend to use the included source code for the kernel Version 2.0.18 (package kernel_src) as the basis for your kernel compilation.

installing compiler
and source code

The following are necessary when you compile the kernel for the first time. The required programs and directories are installed on the hard disk.

```
swinstall -x reinstall=false gcc as86 kernel_src
```

This ensures that the kernel source code (package kernel_src) as well as the packages gcc and as86, both of which are needed for kernel compilation, are installed.

```
cd /usr/src
```

makes this the current directory

```
tar xzvf linux-2.0.18.tar.gz
```

unpacking source code   unpacks the source code of the kernel

```
mv linux-2.0.18 linux
```

moves the source code to the right position

Configuration

Follow these steps with each recompilation:

```
cd /usr/include
rm -rf asm linux scsi
ln -s /usr/src/linux/include/asm-i386 asm
ln -s /usr/src/linux/include/linux linux
ln -s /usr/src/linux/include/scsi scsi
```

This ensures that /usr/include/asm, /usr/include/linux, and /usr/include/scsi are only symbolic links to the kernel source code.

```
cd /usr/src/linux
```

changes to the directory with the kernel source code

```
make mrproper
```

removes the remains of the last compilation

Since kernel Version 1.3.x there have been three variants for the actual configuration:

```
make config
```

> is the conventional variant of the kernel configuration. The user is sequentially prompted for kernel options in a fixed order. You can respond to each prompt with y for yes, n for no, and ? for help. For drivers that are available as modules, you can also enter m for module. If you enter only RETURN, the previous setting is retained (indicated in the prompt by a capital Y, N or M).

```
make menuconfig
```

> provides a more comfortable way to configure the kernel. With the help of text-based, color menus, radio buttons, and dialogs, you can move through various groups of options, request help, and make settings in any order.

```
make xconfig
```

> A faster variant is make xconfig. If you have installed the package tcl7_4, after entering this command line, you can configure the kernel under X Windows with the mouse.

Since you can now get help on the individual options directly during configuration, this will not be handled in detail here.

In general, unnecessary drivers inflate the kernel and might even cause problems. For example, probing for a hardware component that is not present can confuse other components.

If you intend to use the file cache, you should definitely include support for the file cache under file systems in the kernel. This option represents a kernel patch that is not present in the standard kernel distribution.

135

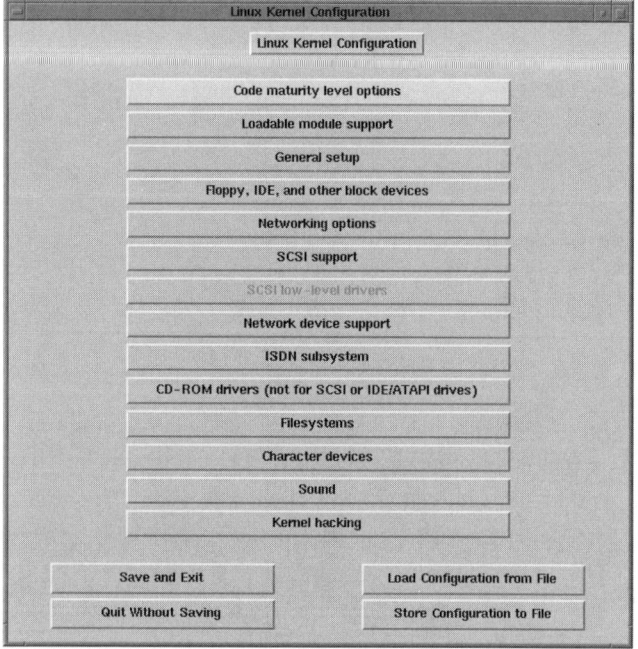

Figure 9.30. Kernel configuration under X11

Dependencies

After configuration, you must determine the dependencies between the parts of the kernel. This occurs as follows:

```
make dep
```

Then you should remove extraneous object files:

```
make clean
```

Compilation

start compilation   Now you can start the actual compilation:

```
make zImage
```

If you have configured parts of the kernel as modules, you need to execute the following command:

```
make modules
```

Detailed information on kernel modules can be found in the file
`/usr/src/linux/Documentation/modules.txt`.

Activation

Finally, activate the new kernel with the command

```
make install
```

and (if applicable) the modules with the command

```
make modules_install
```

The new kernel is then in the file /vmlinuz, and the old one was renamed /vmlinuz.old. Invoking make install again overwrites the backup, however.

The new kernel is activated on the next booting, e.g., initiated with

```
shutdown -r now
```

If problems occur on booting with the new kernel, you can copy the old kernel /vmlinuz.old to /vmlinuz.

reactivate old kernel

9.25   X11 configuration

Installing the X Window System under Linux normally consists of simply unpacking the programs and files from the various tar archives. With most Linux packages this occurs during the installation of the operating system and so it poses no problem. The configuration task grows complicated when the X server must be adapted to the available video board and monitor. Then configuration requires modifying the central configuration file XF86Config, which resides in the directory /etc or /usr/lib/X11.

tar archive

XF86Config

The XF86Config file

This file is divided into sections. Here we list these sections and explain their most important aspects in detail.

*   **Files**—defines the paths required by the X server for the RGB color table and the font directories.
*   **ServerFlags**—sets the server's general flags, including whether the server can be terminated with Ctrl + Alt + Backspace and how the server should react to UNIX signals.

137

- **Keyboard**—defines the connected keyboard and the function of special modifier keys.
- **Pointer**—adapts the mouse driver by specification of its type and the interface used.
- **Monitor**—determines the limit values and the timing data of the monitor(s).
- **Device**—describes video boards.
- **Screen**—assigns monitor, definitions, and video board to an X server.

The files section

font server

Installation packages usually handle the settings for the RGB table and font paths correctly. Font paths can be entered in individual lines or in a single line delimited by commas. Font servers are specified as `transport/hostname:portnumber`, for example, `tcp/zeus:7100`. The following example shows a file section:

```
Section "Files"

RgbPath      "/usr/X11R6/lib/X11/rgb"
# Examples of font server entries:
#    FontPath    "tcp/127.0.0.1:7100"
#    FontPath    "tcp/font.server.de:7100"
     FontPath    "/usr/lib/X11/fonts/misc/"
     FontPath    "/usr/lib/X11/fonts/Type1/"
     FontPath    "/usr/lib/X11/fonts/Speedo/"
     FontPath    "/usr/lib/X11/fonts/75dpi/"
     FontPath    "/usr/lib/X11/fonts/100dpi/"

EndSection
```

The server flags section

debugging

Two options apply in this section. `NoTrapSignal` is only interesting for debugging purposes, and `DontZap` prevents terminating the server with Ctrl + Alt + Backspace :

```
Section "ServerFlags"

# If the following option is activated, the X server dumps
# a core file when it receives a signal.  Here the option is
# disabled as a comment.
#    NoTrapSignals

# Activating the following option disables the key combination
# <Crtl-Alt-BS> to terminate the servers.
```

```
DontZap

EndSection
```

The keyboard section

The keyboard driver is adapted here. Standard protocol should always
be used. In addition, on non-English keyboards, note that the right
Alt key (**AltGr**) must be redefined as ModeShift to allow the use
of special characters such as "@" and "–." Many example files employ
the American keyboard and use the right **Alt** key as Compose.

special characters

```
Section "Keyboard"
Protocol    "Standard"
# Delay and repeat rate for autorepeat
AutoRepeat   500 5
# Numlock to be handled by the server
serverNumLock
# Which LEDs can the user influence (e.g., with xset)
#   Xleds        1 2 3
# Function of modifier keys
    LeftAlt      Meta
    RightAlt     ModeShift
    RightCtl     Compose
#   ScrollLock  ModeLock
# Switching consoles with SysReq (normally not used in Linux)
#   VTSysReq
# Command to be executed on opening of the virtuellen terminal
#   VTInit "command"
EndSection
```

The pointer section

For the mouse driver, it normally suffices to specify the type of mouse
and the interface used. Usually, installation creates a link for this
interface as /dev/mouse/dev/mouse, which can be used here.

mouse

```
Section "Pointer"

# One of the following mouse protocols must be selected.
# This need not correspond to the name of the mouse.
# Most generic mice and many Logitech mice
# use Microsoft protocol:
#   Protocol    "Microsoft"
# All normal bus mice:
#   Protocol    "BusMouse"
# Many new serial Logitech mice use the following
# (also see ChordMiddle):
#   Protocol    "Mouseman"
# Older Logitech mice:
#   Protocol    "Logitech"
# Other mice:
#   Protocol    "MouseSystems"
#   Protocol    "MMSeries"
#   Protocol    "PS/2"
#   Protocol    "MMHitTab"
# The following should *not* be used under Linux:
#   Protocol    "Xqueue"
```

```
#    Protocol   "OSMouse"
Protocol    "Microsoft"

# Mouse interface:
Device       "/dev/mouse"

# BaudRate and SampleRate (only for some Logitech mice)
#     BaudRate    9600
#     SampleRate 150

# Emulation of a 3-button mouse, where 3rd mouse key is
# is simulated by simultaneously pressing left and right
# mouse key.
#     Emulate3Buttons

# ChordMiddle is an option for some 3-button Logitech
# and Mouseman mice.
#     ChordMiddle

# The following resets the DTR line of serial mouse port to 0.
# This option is needed for some MouseSystems mice.
#     ClearDTR
# Some mice also require ClearRTS option, which sets RTS to 0.
#     ClearRTS

EndSection
```

The monitor section

This section has several purposes. It sets the limit values and the timing data of a monitor, and there can be multiple occurrences of the section. Thereby each monitor is assigned an identifier with which it can later be referenced. The limit values are the maximum horizontal

bandwidth   synchronization, the vertical refresh rate, and the bandwidth.

These data can be found in the technical documentation of the monitor. If nothing else is specified, the bandwidth is assumed in MHz, the horizontal synchronization in KHz, and the vertical refresh

protection   rate in Hz. Specifying these values in the configuration serves to protect the monitor. On startup, the server tests whether a specified video mode exceeds the monitor's range and discards the mode if it does.

video modes   After the technical data of a monitor, the section lists various video modes that are adapted to the respective monitor. The definition of video modes is discussed in detail below.

```
Section "Monitor"
Identifier   "VESA Generic Monitor"
VendorName   "Unknown"
    ModelName    "Unknown"
    BandWidth    300
    HorizSync    23-38
VertRefresh 50-60
# 640x480@60Hz Non-Interlaced mode
# Horizontal Sync = 31.5kHz
```

```
ModeLine "640x480" 25 640 664 760 800 480 491 493 525
# 640x480@64Hz Non-Interlaced mode
# Horizontal Sync = 33.7kHz
#ModeLine "640x480" 28 640 664 704 832 480 489 492 525
# VESA 640x480@72Hz Non-Interlaced mode
# Horizontal Sync = 37.9kHz
#ModeLine "640x480" 31.5 640 664 704 832 480 489 492 520
# VESA 800x600@56Hz Non-Interlaced mode
# Horizontal Sync = 35.1kHz
ModeLine "800x600" 36 800 824 896 1024 600 601 603 625
# VESA 800x600@60Hz Non-Interlaced mode
# Horizontal Sync = 37.9kHz
ModeLine "800x600" 40 800 840 968 1056 600 601 605 628
# VESA 800x600@72Hz Non-Interlaced mode
# Horizontal Sync = 48kHz
#ModeLine "800x600" 50 800 856 976 1040 600 637 643 666
# VESA 1024x768@60Hz Non-Interlaced mode
# Horizontal Sync = 48.4kHz
#ModeLine "1024x768" 65 1024 1032 1176 1344 768 771 777 806
# 1024x768@42.6Hz, Interlaced mode
# Horizontal Sync = 34.8kHz
ModeLine "1024x768" 44 1024 1040 1216 1264 768 777 785 817
Interlace
# 1024x768@43.5Hz, Interlaced mode (8514/A standard)
# Horizontal Sync = 35.5kHz
ModeLine "1024x768" 45 1024 1040 1216 1264 768 777 785 817
Interlace
# VESA 1024x768@70Hz Non-Interlaced mode
# Horizontal Sync=56.5kHz
#ModeLine "1024x768" 75 1024 1048 1184 1328 768 771 777 806
# 1024x768@76Hz Non-Interlaced mode
# Horizontal Sync=62.5kHz
#ModeLine "1024x768" 85 1024 1032 1152 1360 768 784 787 823
# 1152x900@60.14Hz, Non-Interlaced mode
# Horizontal Sync=57.4kHz
##ModeLine "1152x900" 85 1152 1192 1384 1480 900 905 923 955
# 1152x900@48.5Hz, Interlaced mode
# Horizontal Sync=45.6kHz
##ModeLine "1152x900" 62 1152 1184 1288 1360 900 898 929 939
Interlace
# 1152x900@48.5Hz, Non-Interlaced mode
# Horizontal Sync=76.1kHz
#ModeLine "1152x900" 110 1152 1284 1416 1536 900 902 905 941
# 1280x1024@44Hz, Interlaced mode
# Horizontal Sync=51kHz
##ModeLine "1280x1024" 80 1280 1296 1512 1568 1024 1025 1037
1165 Interlace
# 1280x1024@61Hz, Non-Interlaced mode
# Horizontal Sync=64.25kHz
##ModeLine "1280x1024" 110 1280 1328 1512 1712 1024 1025 1028
1054
# 1280x1024@70Hz, Non-Interlaced mode
# Horizontal Sync=74.4kHz
#ModeLine "1280x1024" 125 1280 1296 1552 1680 1024 1024 1032
1062
# 1280x1024@74Hz, Non-Interlaced mode
# Horizontal Sync=78.85kHz
#ModeLine "1280x1024" 135 1280 1312 1456 1712 1024 1027 1030
1064
EndSection

Section "Monitor"
Identifier "EIZO FlexScan T660"
VendorName "EIZO"
ModelName "FlexScan T660i-T/TCO"
    BandWidth   135.0
    HorizSync   30.0-82.0
VertRefresh 55.0-90.0
ModeLine "1024x768" 80 1024 1088 1152 1280 768 770 772 778
ModeLine "1280x1024" 135 1280 1328 1408 1688 1024 1025 1026
1060
ModeLine "1536x1152" 168 1536 1616 1760 2048 1152 1154 1158
1188
```

```
EndSection
```

The device section

video board

This section specifies the available video boards. Like Monitor, it can occur repeatedly. For many boards, neither the chipset nor the dot clocks need to be specified, since the server can collect this data automatic ally on startup. For more complicated boards, however, specification becomes necessary.

```
Section "Device"
Identifier   "Generic VGA 16 Color"
#server      "XF86'VGA16"
VendorName   "GENERIC"
BoardName    "GENERIC"
EndSection

Section "Device"
Identifier   "Generic SVGA"
#server      "XF86'SVGA"
VendorName   "GENERIC"
    BoardName    "GENERIC"
    VideoRam     1024
EndSection

Section "Device"
Identifier   "Generic SVGA, VideoRam limited to 1MB"
#server      "XF86'SVGA"
VendorName   "GENERIC"
    BoardName    "GENERIC"
    VideoRam     1024
EndSection

Section "Device"
Identifier "Sigma Legend ET-4000"
#server      "XF86'SVGA"
VendorName "Sigma"
BoardName "Sigma Legend ET-4000"
Option "legend"
EndSection

#From: koenig@tat.physik.uni-tuebingen.de (Harald Koenig)
#Date: Sun, 25 Sep 1994 18:55:42 +0100 (MET)

Section "Device"
Identifier "Miro 10SD GENDAC"
#server      "XF86'S3"
VendorName "MIRO"
BoardName "10SD GENDAC"
#    Clocks  25.255 28.311 31.500  0      40.025 64.982 74.844
#    Clocks  25.255 28.311 31.500 36.093 40.025 64.982 74.844
    ClockChip "s3gendac"
    RamDac    "s3gendac"
EndSection
```

clocks

Even if the server can determine the clock frequencies automatically, sometimes it still makes sense to specify them manually because the detected values are used as an identifier. The definitions of video modes refer to this identifier in the mode lines of the monitor definition. If there should be fluctuations during the detection of the clock frequency and a clock were identified at 49.5 Hz instead of 50, then the X server might not identify the frequency used by a video mode and would thus terminate with an error message.

In addition, the server's automatic detection of clock rates can cause problems with some hardware. Specification of the clock frequencies in a board's definition suppresses automatic detection. To establish the available clock frequencies, remove the `clocks` line from the `Xconfig` file and restart the X server with the option `-probeonly`. The X server then displays the detected clock frequencies and other driver information in text mode and then quits.

computing clocks

The screen section

Each special server (SuperVGA server, monochrome server, S3 server, etc.) can be assigned in this section to a monitor and a video board. When the server starts, it selects the appropriate screen and thus has the data of the video board and the monitor. In addition, this section lists possible video modes that refer to mode lines from the corresponding Monitor section. At run time the user can switch between these modes with the key combinations **Ctrl** + **Alt** + **+** and **Ctrl** + **Alt** + **−** on the numeric keypad.

screen

```
Section "Screen"
Driver "vga256"
Device "Generic SVGA"
Monitor "IDEK VisionMaster 17 (1)"
Subsection "Display"
Moof the "1280x1024" "1024x768" "800x600" "640x480"
EndSubsection
EndSection

Section "Screen"
Driver "accel"
Device "Miro 20SD"
Monitor "IDEK VisionMaster 17 (1)"
Subsection "Display"
Moof the "1024x768" "800x600" "640x480"
EndSubsection
EndSection
```

Setting the video modes

The most difficult and dangerous part of configuration is setting video modes, since this directly defines the synchronization frequencies (timings) of the monitor, and a low-priced monitor, without protective

synchronization

143

circuitry against exceeding its frequency limits, can be damaged by incorrect values. To prevent damage, the frequency limits of the monitor should be entered in the configuration file from the start.

optimization

no flicker

The advantage of this kind of configuration of the video mode is that the available monitor can be used to full advantage. For example, a 14" monitor whose maximum horizontal synchronization frequency (HSF) is too low to display 800 × 600 pixels flicker-free could be operated at a resolution of 800 × 550 with 72 Hz screen refresh rate (RR).

vertical timing

For each mode, the configuration file specifies the clock to be used as well as four values each for horizontal and vertical synchronization. The specification can be in a single line (as ModeLine) or distributed across several lines. The two definitions in the following example are identical:

```
#        Mode  Clock  horizontal              vertical
ModeLine "800x600"   45   800   840 1030 1184   600   600   606
624

# The same mode in a different notation:
Mode "800x600"
    DotClock        45
    HTimings        800 840 1030 1184
    VTimings        600 600 606 624
EndMode
```

interlace mode

As an option, flags can be specified at the end of a mode definition, including `interlace`, `+hsync`, `+vsync`, and `csync`. These flags influence the interlace mode and the type of synchronization.

```
Mode "1024x768i"
    DotClock        45
    HTimings        1024 1048 1208 1264
    VTimings        768 776 784 817
    Flags           "Interlace"
EndMode
```

The values for horizontal timing, in order, are: The respective meanings of the values in each group of four numbers are

- the maximum number of pixels after which the picture ceases to be displayed;

- the number of dot-clock ticks to the start of the horizontal synchronization pulse (sync), whereby the values are counted ongoing;
- the number of dot-clock ticks until the horizontal synchronization pulse ends and the second guard time of the electron beam begins;
- the total number of dot-clock ticks to the end of a cycle (frame).

```
ModeLine "800x5"   45   800 840 1030 1120    540 540 546 558
```

This example defines a mode with a resolution of 800x540 pixels, which is assigned the name "800x5."

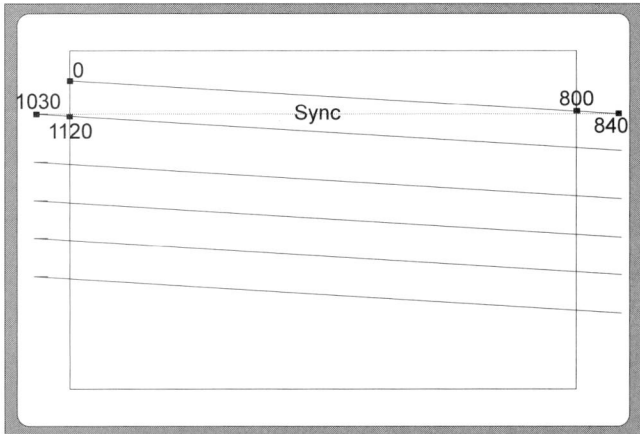

Figure 9.31. Schematic representation of the composition of a screen

The horizontal resolution is 800 pixels, and after the end of a visible line a guard time begins for the electron beam to rest. The guard time lasts until 840 pixels; then the synchronization pulse   sync pulse begins. It lasts 190 dot-clock ticks until 1030. Then there is a guard time until 1120. Thereupon the next horizontal cycle begins. After 540 horizontal cycles (that is, scan lines), the vertical synchronization intervenes, lasting 6 horizontal cycles. Then there is another guard time until the 558th cycle. After the guard time, the next screen starts.

The files `video.tutorial` and `VideoModes.doc` in the directory `/usr/lib/X11/doc` describe in depth the rules for

determination of values determining the exact values for such a video mode.

However, it is often simpler to find a corresponding entry in one of the many example files and to modify it. There

spreadsheet is also a table for the simple spreadsheet program `sc`, which simplifies the computation of the values. This can be found on the FTP server `sunsite.unc.edu` and its mirror servers in the directory `/pub/Linux/X11/install` with the file name `modegen.taz`.

The limiting factor for simple monitors is usually the maximum

horizontal timing horizontal synchronization frequency. This is the frequency with which the electron beam moves from left to right and from scan

computation line to scan line. This frequency is computed by dividing the driving clock rate, specified in MHz, by the largest (right) number of the block for horizontal timing:

$$f_{horizontal} = \frac{f_{pixel}}{N_{pixel}}$$

In the above example, the required horizontal sweep frequency would be 45 MHz / 1120, or approximately 40 KHz. This is the upper limit for the monitor in our example.

Refresh rate

To compute the vertical synchronization frequency (vertical timing or

computation screen refresh rate), divide the horizontal synchronization frequency by the number of scan lines (i.e., horizontal cycles) necessary for a complete screen. This is the rightmost number in the block for vertical timing.

$$f_{vertical} = \frac{f_{horizontal}}{N_{scan\ lines}}$$

In our example we have 40 KHz/558, or 72 Hz. If 600 lines rather than 540 are to be displayed, then the vertical synchronization frequency falls significantly below 72 Hz, which the user notices as light flicker ing of the monitor.

With a better monitor whose maximum horizontal synchronization frequency is, for example, 60 KHz, and a newer video board that offers a faster clock, the driving clock frequency could be raised to achieve a higher refresh rate.

To modify an existing video mode, we recommend copying and modifying the mode repeatedly and entering each modified mode in a mode line of the Screen section with a different name. Then start the X server and compare the effects of the modifications by switching modes with Ctrl + Alt and the + or – key on the numerical keypad. If the monitor no longer synchronizes with a new mode, i.e., it fails to show a stable picture, quickly change modes or end the X server with Ctrl + Alt + Backspace to avoid damage to the monitor.

The program vgaset provides a valuable aid in adjusting the picture. Started in an xterm, it permits interactive manipulation of the picture position. At the touch of a key the borders can be increased or decreased, and the duration of the synchronization signal can be changed. The eight values to be entered for the current settings in the file Xconfig are constantly displayed.

Keyboard layout configuration

The X Window System manages the keyboard independently of the kernel. An American keyboard is initialized as the default. Country-specific keyboard tables can be loaded with the utility xmodmap. When the X server is launched in a normal configuration, xmodmap is invoked with the file .Xmodmap. The utility seeks this file first in the user's home directory and then in the directory /usr/lib/X11/xinit.

If a given keyboard layout is to be modified systemwide, it must be adapted in the directory /usr/lib/X11/xinit. Ready .Xmodmap files are included in some distributions, or they can be drawn from FTP servers such as sunsite.unc.edu in the directory /pub/Linux/X11/misc.

Since xmodmap is normally invoked in an xinitrc script, the invocation might need to be modified to seek the file .Xmodmap in

---

flicker

better performance

copying a mode

avoid damage

vgaset

xmodmap

xinitrc

another directory or under another name. In case of doubt, examine the script that starts the X server, usually `startx`.

xkeycaps
Using the `xkeycaps` utility certainly proves to be a more comfortable alternative. It is included in many Linux distributions and can be found on the usual FTP servers. This program offers an X11 user interface (see Figure 9.32). The user can display the current keyboard layout and interactively change it with the mouse.

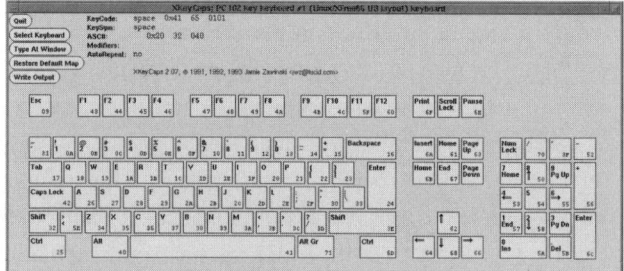

Figure 9.32. `xkeycaps`

American Linux distributions frequently lack other country-specific keyboard layouts. Hence we give an example of a German `.Xmodmap` as an example of country-specific keyboard adaptation. Note the keyboard symbol number 12, which is often erroneously
paragraph   configured with the symbol `paragraph` instead of `section`.

```
keycode    8 =
keycode    9 = Escape
keycode   10 = 1 exclam
keycode   11 = 2 quotedbl twosuperior
keycode   12 = 3 section threesuperior
keycode   13 = 4 dollar
keycode   14 = 5 percent
keycode   15 = 6 ampersand
keycode   16 = 7 slash braceleft
keycode   17 = 8 parenleft bracketleft
keycode   18 = 9 parenright bracketright
keycode   19 = 0 equal braceright
keycode   20 = ssharp question backslash
keycode   21 = apostrophe grave
keycode   22 = BackSpace
keycode   23 = Tab
keycode   24 = q Q at
keycode   25 = W
keycode   26 = E
keycode   27 = R
keycode   28 = T
keycode   29 = Z
```

```
keycode  30 = U
keycode  32 = O
keycode  33 = P
keycode  34 = Udiaeresis
keycode  35 = plus asterisk asciitilde
keycode  36 = Return
keycode  37 = Control`L
keycode  38 = A
keycode  39 = S
keycode  40 = D
keycode  41 = F
keycode  42 = G
keycode  43 = H
keycode  44 = J
keycode  45 = k K Arabic`kaf
keycode  46 = l L Arabic`lam Greek`lambda
keycode  47 = Odiaeresis
keycode  48 = Adiaeresis
keycode  49 = asciicircum degree
keycode  50 = Shift`L
keycode  51 = numbersign apostrophe
keycode  52 = Y
keycode  53 = X
keycode  54 = C
keycode  55 = V
keycode  56 = B
keycode  57 = N
keycode  58 = m M mu
keycode  59 = comma semicolon
keycode  60 = period colon
keycode  61 = minus underscore
keycode  62 = Shift`R
keycode  63 = KP`Multiply
keycode  64 = Alt`L
keycode  65 = space
keycode  66 = Caps`Lock
keycode  67 = F1
keycode  68 = F2
keycode  69 = F3
keycode  70 = F4
keycode  71 = F5
keycode  72 = F6
keycode  73 = F7
keycode  74 = F8
keycode  75 = F9
keycode  76 = F10
keycode  77 = Num`Lock
keycode  78 = Scroll`Lock
keycode  79 = Home KP`7 KP`7 Home
keycode  80 = Up KP`8 KP`8 Up
keycode  81 = Prior KP`9 KP`9 Prior
keycode  82 = KP`Subtract
keycode  83 = Left KP`4 KP`4 Left
keycode  84 = Begin KP`5 KP`5 Begin
keycode  85 = Right KP`6 KP`6 Right
keycode  86 = KP`Add
keycode  87 = End KP`1 KP`1 End
keycode  88 = Down KP`2 KP`2 Down
keycode  89 = Next KP`3 KP`3 Next
keycode  90 = Insert KP`0 KP`0 Insert
keycode  91 = Delete KP`Decimal KP`Decimal Delete
keycode  92 = 0x1007ff00
keycode  93 =
keycode  94 = less greater bar
keycode  95 = F11
keycode  96 = F12
keycode  97 = Home
keycode  98 = Up
keycode  99 = Prior
keycode 100 = Left
keycode 101 = Begin
keycode 102 = Right
keycode 103 = End
```

```
keycode 104 = Down
keycode 105 = Next
keycode 106 = Insert
keycode 107 = Delete
keycode 108 = KP'Enter
keycode 109 = Control'R
keycode 110 = Pause
keycode 111 = Print
keycode 112 = KP'Divide
keycode 113 = Mode'switch
keycode 114 = Break
```

German X11 keyboard layout adaptation

9.26   Configuration of X applications

application defaults

Most X clients come with an *application defaults* file that is copied into the X11 system region (/usr/lib/X11/app-defaults). This file contains the important default settings for the application, such as size, position, and color of graphical objects and error messages in the respective country-specific language.

class names

Every application was assigned a class name by its programmer that corresponds to the name of its resource file. Class names always begin with a capital letter. Change the background color of xterm (class name XTerm) in the file /usr/lib/X11/app-defaults/XTerm.

XFILESEARCHPATH

Various environment variables (XFILESEARCHPATH, XAPPLERESDIR) affect the search path for resource files. XFILESEARCHPATH allows specification of multiple search paths delimited by colons and handles several special characters as follows:

%C	value of customization resource (*.customization)
%L	language, local codeset
%l	language
%N	class name
%T	file type (app-defaults)

A useful definition of this variable could be as follows:

```
XFILESEARCHPATH=/usr/lib/X11/%T:/usr/local/%T/%N:$HOME/%T/%N
```

Resource files will now be searched for in three directories:

1. /usr/lib/X11/app-defaults/<Class>
2. /usr/local/app-defaults/<Class>
3. <Home-directory>/app-defaults/<Class>

Another way to configure X11 applications is the command xrdb, which loads the passed resource file into one of the properties (RESOURCE_MANAGER or SCREEN_RESOURCES) of the X server. A *property* is a global memory region in the X server which can be assigned a name. On launching of an X application, the resource manager evaluates the resource definitions contained in these properties. Configuring applications by means of resource properties particularly makes sense if applications are started on another computer and the local look and feel is to be affected. xrdb has a number of parameters:

xrdb

property

-all	Operation refers to both properties
-screen	Operation refers only to the property SCREEN_RESOURCES
-global	Operation refers only to the property RESOURCE_MANAGER
query	Displays current contents of a property
merge <file>	Merges contents of a file with a property
edit <file>	Saves contents of a property to a file
remove	Removes a complete property
load <file>	Overwrites a property with contents of a file

xrdb commands

In addition, users can create their own .Xdefaults files in their home directories and thus override the global default settings.

.Xdefaults

The following list gives an overview of the files and paths that are processed sequentially to determine the current widget attributes on starting an application. If a resource is assigned a value at more than one location, then only the last defined value applies.

widget attribute

- Within an application:
  1. Fallback resources
- Application-specific:

151

1. `/usr/lib/$LANG/app-defaults/<class>`
2. `/usr/lib/X11/app-defaults/<class>`

- New search path:
  1. `$XFILESEARCHPATH`
- User-specific:
  1. `$XUSERFILESEARCHPATH`
  2. `$XAPPLRESDIR/$LANG/<class>`
  3. `$XAPPLRESDIR/<class>`
  4. `$HOME/$LANG/<class>`
  5. `$HOME/<class>`
- Screen-specific:
  1. `SCREEN_RESOURCES` property (`xrdb`)
- Display-specific:
  1. `RESOURCE_MANAGER` property (`xrdb`)
  2. `$HOME/.Xdefaults` file
- Host-specific:
  1. `$XENVIRONMENT` variables
  2. `$HOME/.Xdefaults-<hostname>`
- Command line:
  1. Command-line options

Widget attributes

resource values These resource values are represented in ASCII format. To distinguish them within a resource file, the programmer assigns each application a name (class), which seldom corresponds to the program file (instance). Likewise each widget and widget attribute that is externally configurable has a name and belongs to a class. To uniquely reference a widget, the name does not suffice. Instead, as widget path with a file system, this requires a path that represents an excerpt from the widget hierarchy.

To allow manipulation of the attributes of multiple widgets wildcards simultaneously, wildcards (?, *) are permitted in the path. The following is the exact syntax of the resource specification:

```
object.subobject[.subobject...].attribute:
value
```

The individual elements have the following meanings:

object	class or name of program
subobject	class or name of widget
attribute	resource name
value	value

.	delimiter
*	wildcard, any number of, or no, names
?	wildcard, any individual name

The first column of the resource file specifies the attribute to be manipulated. This usually corresponds to a widget resource. However, the programmer can define new, application-specific resources. The hierarchy and the names of the available resources can be taken from the respective Manual page.

attribute

```
Xterm*background:        gray90
XTerm*ScrollBar:         true
XTerm*Foreground:        white
XTerm*Background:        gray20
XTerm*IconName:          XTerm
XTerm*WaitForMap:        true
XTerm*MarginBell:        false
XTerm*JumpScroll:        true
```

Excerpt from a resource file

Likewise, individual widget attributes can be collected into class es. Making use of class identifiers can make a resource file significantly shorter and more readable. The attributes cursor-Color and pointerColor of xterms both belong to the class Foreground. Therefore the following:

```
XTerm*foreground:        green
XTerm*cursorColor:       green
XTerm*pointerColor:      green
```

can be abbreviated as:

```
xterm*Foreground:        green
```

153

editres

Releases 5 and 6 of the X Window System contain an interactive resource manager (editres) that permits comfortable manipulation of all resource values of a running program and saves them on demand to an ASCII file. It is particularly noteworthy that this can be done at run time. Thus the user gets immediate feedback

protocol

on the effects of changes. Unfortunately, the editres protocol is not yet supported by all widget sets, which naturally restricts the use of the tool. The generated ASCII files can easily be integrated into available resource files or appended to the .Xdefaults file.

Configuration of the window manager

The user can configure not just the look of individual applications, but of most X window managers as well. Since many Linux users

fvwm

probably use fvwm, we go into detail only on this window manager. The parameters of thiswindow managerindow manager are set in the file system.fvwmrc in the directory /usr/lib/X11/fvwm. Alternatively, each user can provide a file named .fvwmrc in the user's home directory.

M4 preprocessor

Using the M4 preprocessor provides additional flexibility. This allows linking additional configuration files or testing conditions, for example. The main file (system.fvwmrc) thus becomes relatively comprehensible.

```
################################################################
#
# system.fvwmrc - fvwm configuration
#

################################################################
# Paths

ModulePath /usr/lib/X11/fvwm/modules
PixmapPath /usr/lib/X11/pixmaps:/usr/local/lib/pixmaps
IconPath   /usr/include/X11/bitmaps/

################################################################
# External configuration files

include(/usr/lib/X11/fvwm/fvwm.options)

include(/usr/lib/X11/fvwm/fvwm.menus)

include(/usr/lib/X11/fvwm/fvwm.functions)

include(/usr/lib/X11/fvwm/fvwm.bindings)

include(/usr/lib/X11/fvwm/fvwm.styles)

include(/usr/lib/X11/fvwm/fvwm.goodstuff)
```

```
include(/usr/lib/X11/fvwm/fvwm.modules)

################################################################
# Initialization and restart function

Function "InitFunction"
    Module   "I"    GoodStuff
    Module   "I"    FvwmPager 0 1
    Exec     "I"    exec xterm -sb -sl 400 -geometry +75+390 &
    Exec     "I"    xsetroot -solid LightSlateGray
EndFunction

Function "RestartFunction"
    Module   "I"    GoodStuff
    Exec     "I"    xsetroot -solid LightSlateGray
    Module   "I"    FvwmPager 0 1
EndFunction
```

system.fvwmrc

In addition to definitions for color and font, the file **fvwm.options**
fvwm.options contains a number of other options that determine
the look and feel.

```
################################################################
#
# fvwm.options - general options
#

DeskTopSize 2x2
DeskTopScale 32

# Standard colors
StdForeColor        Black
StdBackColor        #d3d3d3

# Window colors
HiForeColor         Black
HiBackColor         #5f9ea0
StickyForeColor     Black
StickyBackColor     #60c0a0

# Menu colors
MenuForeColor       Black
MenuBackColor       grey
MenuStippleColor    SlateGrey

# Fonts
Font                -adobe-helvetica-medium-r-*-*-12-*-*-*-*-*-*-*
WindowFont          -adobe-helvetica-bold-r-*-*-12-*-*-*-*-*-*-*
IconFont            fixed

# Rectangles in which icons are positioned
IconBox 5 -80 -140 -5
IconBox 5 -160 -140 -85
IconBox 5 -240 -140 -165
IconBox 5 -320 -140 -245

# Motif look and feel
MWMFunctionHints
MWMHintOverride
MWMDecorHints
MWMBorders
MWMButtons
```

```
# Moves all windows with contents
OpaqueMove 100

# Suppress automatic desktop change
EdgeScroll 0 0

# Delay in changing desktop section
EdgeResistance 250 50

NoPPosition

# Automatic positioning of new window
RandomPlacement

# Forces decoration in transient shell
DecorateTransients
```

fvwm.options

fvwm.menus The user can create new menus and assign them to a user action.

```
###############################################################
#
# fvwm.menus - Menu configuration
#

Popup "Shells"
        Title    "Shells"
        Exec     "MXterm"          exec mxterm &
        Exec     "Color XTerm"     exec color`xterm &
        Exec     "Rxvt"            exec rxvt &
EndPopup

Popup "Editors"
        Title    "Editors"
        Exec     "GNU emacs"       exec emacs &
        Exec     "NEdit"           exec nedit &
        Exec     "Textedit"        exec textedit &
EndPopup

Popup "Graphics"
        Title    "Graphics / Viewer"
        Exec     "XPaint"          exec xpaint &
        Exec     "XV"              exec xv &
EndPopup

Popup "Modules"
        Title    "Modules"
        Module   "GoodStuff"       GoodStuff
        Module   "Identify"        FvwmIdent
        Module   "SaveDesktop"     FvwmSave
        Module   "Pager"           FvwmPager 0 1
        Module   "FvwmWinList"     FvwmWinList
        Module   "FvwmIconBox"     FvwmIconBox
EndPopup

Popup "Window Ops"
        Title    "Window Ops     "
        Move     "&Move   Alt+F7"
        Resize   "&Size   Alt+F8"
        Lower    "&Lower Alt+F3"
        Raise    "Raise     "
        Stick    " (Un)Stick       "
        Iconify  " (Un)Mi&nimize   Alt+F9"
        Maximize " (Un)Ma&ximize  Alt+F10"
        Maximize " (Un)Maximize Vertical "  0 100
        Nop      "  "
```

```
        Destroy "&Kill   Alt+F4"
        Delete  "Delete
EndPopup

Popup "Window Ops2"
        Move    "&Move   Alt+F7"
        Resize  "&Size   Alt+F8"
        Iconify " (Un)Mi&nimize  Alt+F9"
        Maximize "(Un)Ma&ximize Alt+F10"
        Lower   "&Lower Alt+F3"
        Nop     " "
        Destroy "&Kill   Alt+F4"
        Delete  "Delete "
        Nop     " "
        Module          "ScrollBar"      FvwmScroll 2 2
EndPopup

###############################################################
#
# Mainmenu

Popup "Programs"
        Title   "Programs"
        Exec    "Xterm"                  exec xterm -sb -sl 400
&
        Popup   "Shells"                 Shells
        Popup   "Editors"                Editors
        Popup   "Graphics"               Graphics
        Popup   "Modules"                Modules
        Exec    "Screen Lock"            exec xlock &
        Nop     " "
        Restart "Restart Fvwm"           fvwm
        Quit    "Exit"
EndPopup
```

fvwm.menus

Within the configuration file of fvwm, new functions can be defined that are usually assigned to a keyboard or mouse action.

```
###############################################################
#
# fvwm.functions - function definition
#
Function "Move-or-Raise"
        Move            "Motion"
        Raise           "Motion"
        Raise           "Click"
        RaiseLower      "DoubleClick"
EndFunction

Function "maximize func"
        Maximize        "Motion" 0 100
        Maximize        "Click" 0 80
        Maximize        "DoubleClick" 100 100
EndFunction

Function "window ops func"
        PopUp   "Click"        Window Ops2
        PopUp   "Motion"       Window Ops2
EndFunction

Function "Move-or-Lower"
        Move            "Motion"
        Lower           "Motion"
```

```
         Lower           "Click"
         RaiseLower      "DoubleClick"
EndFunction

Function "Move-or-Iconify"
         Move            "Motion"
         Iconify         "DoubleClick"
EndFunction

Function "Resize-or-Raise"
         Resize          "Motion"
         Raise           "Motion"
         Raise           "Click"
         RaiseLower      "DoubleClick"
EndFunction
```

fvwm.functions

fvwm.bindings   The file `fvwm.bindings` contains the mappings between mouse and keyboard actions and the associated actions.

```
###############################################################
#
# fvwm.bindings - keyboard- and mouse configuration
#
# Structure of a configuration line:
#
#       <key>        <context>  <modifier>  <function>
#
#       <key>        (mouse) key
#       <context>    R - root window
#                    W - application window
#                    T - title bar
#                    S - window sides
#                    F - window frame
#                    I - icon
#                    A - everything but title bar
#                    0,1,2,...  - window element
#       <modifier>   N - no modifier key
#                    A - alternate
#                    C - control
#                    M - meta
#                    S - shift
#                    mod1-mod5 - X11 modifiers
#       <function>   fvwm function
#
# mouse click on root window
Mouse 1    R        A        PopUp "Programs"
Mouse 2    R        A        PopUp "Window Ops"
Mouse 3    R        A        Module "FvwmWinList" FvwmWinList
Transient

# window element
Mouse 0    1        A        Function "window`ops`func"
Mouse 0    2        A        Function "maximize`func"
Mouse 0    4        A        Iconify
Mouse 1    F        A        Function "Resize-or-Raise"
Mouse 1    TS       A        Function "Move-or-Raise"

# icon actions
Mouse 1    I        A        Function "Move-or-Iconify"
Mouse 2    I        A        Iconify

# window operations
```

```
Mouse 2   FST     A     Function "window'ops'func"
Mouse 3   TSTF    A     RaiseLower

# keyboard shortcut
Key F1    A       M     Popup "Window Ops"
Key F2    A       M     Popup "Programs"
Key F3    A       M     Lower
Key F4    A       M     Destroy
Key F5    A       M     CirculateUp
Key F6    A       M     CirculateDown
Key F7    A       M     Move
Key F8    A       M     Resize
Key F9    A       M     Iconify
Key F10   A       M     Maximize
```

fvwm.bindings

The file `fvwm.styles` establishes the look and feel of individual applications.   fvwm.styles

```
################################################################
#
# fvwm.styles - Style configuration
#
Style "*"             BorderWidth 7, HandleWidth 5
Style "FvwmPager"     Sticky, NoTitle
Style "FvwmBanner"    StaysOnTop
Style "GoodStuff"     Sticky, WindowListSkip, NoTitle
Style "xterm"         Icon terminal.xpm
Style "xcalc"         Icon rcalc.xpm
Style "xman"          Icon xman.xpm
Style "xvgr"          Icon graphs.xpm
Style "Mail"          Icon sndmail.xpm
Style "emacs*"        Icon editor2.xpm
```

fvwm.styles

Each of the `fvwm` modules has its own configuration possibilities, which are summarized in the file `fvwm.modules`.   fvwm.modules

```
################################################################
#
# fvwm.modules - Module configuration
#
################### Window identifier ####################
*FvwmIdentBack MidnightBlue
*FvwmIdentFore Yellow
*FvwmIdentFont -adobe-helvetica-medium-r-*-*-12-*-*-*-*-*-*-*

################### FvwmWinList ###########################
*FvwmWinListBack #d3d3d3
*FvwmWinListFore Black
*FvwmWinListFont -adobe-helvetica-bold-r-*-*-10-*-*-*-*-*-*-*
*FvwmWinListAction Click1 Iconify -1,Focus
*FvwmWinListAction Click2 Iconify
*FvwmWinListAction Click3 Module "FvwmIdent" FvwmIdent
*FvwmWinListUseSkipList
*FvwmWinListGeometry +0-1
```

```
####################### FvwmIconBox ##########################
*FvwmIconBoxIconBack    #cfcfcf
*FvwmIconBoxIconHiFore   black
*FvwmIconBoxIconHiBack   #5f9ea0
*FvwmIconBoxBack    #cfcfcf
*FvwmIconBoxFore    blue
*FvwmIconBoxGeometry    1x5+0+89
*FvwmIconBoxMaxIconSize 64x38
*FvwmIconBoxFont
-adobe-helvetica-medium-r-*-*-12-*-*-*-*-*-*-*
*FvwmIconBoxSortIcons
*FvwmIconBoxPadding     4
*FvwmIconBoxLines    10
*FvwmIconBoxPlacement        Top Left
#
# mouse bindings
#
*FvwmIconBoxMouse    1        Click         RaiseLower
*FvwmIconBoxMouse    1        DoubleClick   Iconify
*FvwmIconBoxMouse    2        Click         Iconify -1, Focus
*FvwmIconBoxMouse    3        Click         Module
"FvwmIdent" ndings
#
# Key bindings
#
*FvwmIconBoxKey      r        RaiseLower
*FvwmIconBoxKey      space    Iconify
*FvwmIconBoxKey      d        Close
#
# FvwmIconBox built-in functions
#
*FvwmIconBoxKey      n        Next
*FvwmIconBoxKey      p        Prev
*FvwmIconBoxKey      h        Left
*FvwmIconBoxKey      j             Down
*FvwmIconBoxKey      k             Up
*FvwmIconBoxKey      l             Right
#
# Icon file specifications
#
*FvwmIconBox    "*"              unknown1.xpm
*FvwmIconBox    "Mosaic"         www-shape.xpm
*FvwmIconBox    "xterm"          terminal.xpm
*FvwmIconBox    "GoodStuff"      toolbox.xpm
*FvwmIconBox    "*ircon*"        daffy.xpm
*FvwmIconBox    "*anual*"        xman.xpm

########################## Pager ############################
*FvwmPagerBack #908090
*FvwmPagerFore #484048
*FvwmPagerFont -adobe-helvetica-bold-r-*-*-10-*-*-*-*-*-*-*
*FvwmPagerHilight #cab3ca
*FvwmPagerGeometry 0+0
*FvwmPagerLabel 0 Strobel
*FvwmPagerLabel 1 Uhl
*FvwmPagerSmallFont 5x8
```

fvwm.modules

fvwm.goodstuff

The configuration of the GoodStuff module resides in its own
file, named fvwm.goodstuff. GoodStuff enables including the
most important applications in an icon bar. A click on an icon
launches the corresponding program. The Swallow option enables
depicting programs like xload and xclock in the icon bar.

```
################################################################
#
# fvwm.goodstuff - Goodstuff configuration

*GoodStuffBack gray60
*GoodStuffGeometry 65x715-1+0
*GoodStuffColumns 1
*GoodStuffFont -adobe-helvetica-medium-r-*-*-12-*-*-*-*-*-*-*

#            Name     Icon          Action   WindowTitle command

*GoodStuff " "        " "           Swallow "xclock"    xclock
-bg gray60 &
*GoodStuff " "        " "           Swallow "xload"     xload
-bg gray60 &
*GoodStuff " "        " "           Swallow "xbiff"     xbiff
-bg gray60 &
*GoodStuff XTerm      terminal.xpm  Exec "xterm"        xterm
-sb -sl 400 &
*GoodStuff NetScape   www.xpm       Exec "Netscape"
netscape &
*GoodStuff Xman       xman.xpm      Exec "Manual Page"  xman
-bothshow -notopbox &
*GoodStuff Mail       sndmail.xpm   Exec "Mail"         xterm
-T Mail -e pine &
*GoodStuff Emacs      editor.xpm    Exec "emacs"        emacs &
*GoodStuff Exit       lbolt.xpm     Quit
```

fvwm.goodstuff

The above classification of the fvwm configuration is not absolutely necessary. However, it does add some structure to the otherwise incomprehensible configuration file system.fvwmrc.

system.fvwmrc

9.27   The source code CD

On the source code CD you will find the source code of most applications that are part of **Linux Universe**, as well as some interesting demo versions of commercial software.

The source code is in .tar.gz format. The source code of programs in /usr/bin are on the source code CD in the directory usr.bin, and analogously for /usr/lib.

Copy the respective source code file from the CD to /usr/local/src. Then apply the command

```
tar -xvzf <filename>
```

to the file. A separate subdirectory for the application is created automatically where the source code is unpacked.

Compiling the source code

Since all source codes have their own `Makefile`, to compile a program you only need to change to the respective directory and enter `make`.

This automatically launches the complete compilation process. However, some applications also have an `IMakefile`. Here the commands `xmkmf` and `make Makefile` or `make Makefiles` generate the actual `Makefile`, to which the `make` command is then applied. Refer to the Manual Page for `xmkmf` and the READMEs of the respective application.

Reference

---

apropos terms

Searches the command descriptions in the Manual pages for the terms passed as parameters and displays the descriptions of the appropriate commands. This is equivalent to the command man -k. (Also see whatis.)

---

ar [-] operation [arguments] [position_name] archive [files]

Processes an archive file, which is usually a C compiler library. With this command you can combine any binary files to a library or extract files from a library. Only one operation may be specified, but multiple arguments are permitted.

Available operations

d   deletes the files from the archive

m   moves the files to the archive (with the position depending on additional arguments)

p   lists the files in the archive

q   appends the specified files to the end of the archive

r   replaces the specified files in the archive with the new files

t   lists the contents of an archive (with argument v providing a verbose list output)

x   extracts all files or only those specified from the archive

Available arguments

a	places the `files` in the `archive` after `position` name (can be specified with `r` or `m`)
b	places the files in the `archive` before `position` name (can be specified with `r` or `m`)
c	creates the `archive`
i	see argument `b`
o	retains the original file date on extraction
s	creates the file table of the `archive` anew
u	replaces only files that have been modified (can be specified with `r`)
v	outputs detailed messages for every operation

---

at [options] time

at

Executes commands at a certain `time`. The commands are entered at the standard input device and terminated with EOF (⌈**Ctrl**⌋+⌈**d**⌋). Option `f` permits alternative input from a shell script. A Bourne shell (`/bin/sh`) is used for execution.

Via the option `q` individual jobs can be assigned to different queues (a-z, A-Z), where letters later in the alphabet reflect decreasing priority.

The `time` can be specified in numeric form (HHMM, HH:MM) or with a keyword such as `noon`, `teatime` (16:00) or `midnight`. Alternatively, the `time` can be specified as a difference such as `now +3 hours`. Minutes, hours, days, weeks, months, and years are permissible units. If the job is to run on a certain day, then the month (Jan, Feb, Mar, ...) and the year (95, 96, ...) are specified additionally.

Available options

-b	equivalent to the command `batch`
-d	removes the specified jobs from the queue (`atrm`)
-f *file*	executes the commands in *file*
-l	lists the current user's jobs (`atq`)

-m sends an e-mail to the user when the commands have been completed

-q *Q* assigns a job to a particular queue specified in *Q* (a-z, A-Z)

-V returns the version number

---

atq [options]

Displays the jobs that are yet to be executed by the user's at commands.

atq

Available options

-q *Q* restricts output to the contents of a specific queue *Q*

-V displays the version number of the command

-v displays a list of jobs that have been executed, but not deleted

---

atrm [options] jobs

Removes the specified at jobs. A job is identified by its job ID, displayed by the at or atq command.

atrm

Available options

-V displays the version number

---

awk [options] [program] [-v Var=value ...]
[files]

awk is a simple interpreter with the combined functionality of grep and sed. It contains its own C-like language. awk is particularly suitable for evaluating ASCII files and for creating scripts for system administration.

awk

Available options

-f *file* reads the program from the specified file instead of the command line

-F *c* sets the delimiting character for fields to c

-v *var=value* assigns the variable var the specified value

basename pathname [suffix]

Clears the path and optionally a specified file extension and outputs the remaining file names to the standard output device. It is usually used in shell scripts.

bash [options] [arguments]

A command interpreter similar to Bourne shell and Korn shell.

batch [options] [time]

Behaves like the at command. However, it only executes the specified commands when the system load is low. (Also see at.)

Available options

-f *file*   executes the commands specified in *file*

-m   sends an e-mail to the user when the commands have been completed

-q *Q*   assigns the job to the queue specified in *Q* (a-z, A-Z)

-V   displays the version number

bc [options] [files]

Interactive program for computation numbers to another base. bc has its own language, which supports the definition of new functions, for example.

Available options

-l   makes the functions of the mathematics library available

-s   causes POSIX-compatible behavior

-w   displays warnings that conform to POSIX

Example

```
zeus:/home/uh1> bc
bc 1.02 (Mar3, 92) Copyright © 1991, 1992 Free Software Foundation, Inc.
This is free software with ABSOLUTLY NO WARRANTY.
For details type 'warranty'.
a=5
b=3
```

```
a*b
15
quit
zeus:/home/uhl>
```

cal [options] [[month] year]

Displays a calendar for the current month or a specified month or year. The number of the year must be given in long form (e.g., 1995) and the month as a number (1–12).

Available options

-j   displays a Julian calendar (with days numbered sequentially)

-y   displays a calendar for the current year

cat [options] [files]

Reads multiple files and outputs them to the standard output device. If no files are specified, the standard input device is read. For this command, output is frequently redirected with >.

Available options

-b   sequentially numbers all nonempty lines

-e   can be specified along with -v and outputs "$" for end of line (EOL)

-n   sequentially numbers all lines

-s   replaces a group of blank lines with a single one

-u   unbuffered output

-v   also outputs control characters and other nonprintable characters

-t   can be specified along with -v and outputs "^I" instead of tabs and "^L" instead of page feeds

Example

```
zeus:/home/uhl> cat >file.txt
This is the contents of the file!
<Ctrl-d>
zeus:/home/uhl> cat file.txt
This is the content of the file!
zeus:/home/uhl>
```

cc [options] files

C compiler (see gcc).

---

cd [directory]

Changes the current directory. This command is usually included in the shell. If no directory is specified, the current user's home directory is assumed by default. Specifying "-" returns to the previous directory.

---

chgrp [options] group files

Changes the group membership of files. This command can be used by the system administrator or by the owner of the specified files. The group can be specified in the form of a numeric group ID or as the name of a group.

Available options

-c   displays the names of the files whose group member-
           ship actually changed
-f   suppresses error messages
-R   changes the group membership of files in subdirecto-
           ries (recursively)
-v   describes each change in a verbose manner

---

chmod [options] permissions files

Changes the permissions of the specified files. This command can be used by the system administrator or the owner of the specified files. The permissions can be specified numerically (octal format) or with a command string. The command string can consist of: the designation for owner (u), group (g), or other (o); the command to add (+), remove (-), or set (=); the permissions to read (r), write (w), or execute (x); and the commands to set or reset the special flags *set user ID* (s) and *sticky* (t).

Available options

-c   displays the names of files whose permissions actually changed

-f   suppresses error messages

-R   also changes the permissions of files in subdirectories (recursively)

-v   describes each change in a verbose manner

Examples

```
chmod u+x file
```
        adds execution permission for the owner of the file
```
chmod go-wx files
```
        removes read and execution permissions for the specified files for the group and other users
```
chmod g+s file
```
        sets the *set group ID* flag of the specified file
```
chmod=r file
```
        sets the file's permissions to read-only for everyone
```
chmod 644 file
```
        allows read and write permissions for the owner and read permissions for all others

---

chown [options] owner [:−.group] files

Changes the owner and optionally the group as well for the specified files. The owner and the group can be specified as numeric IDs or as names.

chown

Available options

-c   displays the names of the files whose owner has actually changed

-f   suppresses error messages

-R   also recursively changes owners of files in subdirectories

-v   describes each change in a verbose manner

cksum [files]

Computes CRC checksums for the specified files and displays these along with their file size and file name.

clear

Clears the screen.

cmp [options] file1 [file2]

Compares the contents of two files bytewise. If the files are identical, 0 is returned; otherwise, 1. If "-" is specified as the file name, then the command reads from the standard input device. The same applies if file2 is not specified.

Available options

-c	displays the characters that are different
-l	displays the offset and octal values of deviating bytes
-s	suppresses all screen output

comm [options] file1 file2

Compares two linewise presorted files. Without additional options the output is in three columns: the first column contains the lines that occur only in file1, the second column displays all lines that occur exclusively in file2, and the third column contains all common lines.

Available options

-1	suppresses column 1
-2	suppresses column 2
-3	suppresses column 3

compress [options] [files]

Compresses the specified files using the Lempel-Ziv method. The compression is indicated by appending ".Z" to the file name. All other file attributes are retained.

Available options

-b *n* restricts to *n* the number of bits that may be used for coding
-c outputs the results to the standard output device and does not change any files
-f compresses without confirmation if the target file already exists
-r also compresses files in subdirectories (recursively)
-v provides a verbose status report
-V displays the version number of the program

---

cp [options] file1 file2
cp [options] files directory

Copies file1 to file2 or the specified files into the directory. If the target file (file2) already exists, it is overwritten (although option -i requires confirmation).

Available options

-a combination of -d, -p and -r
-b creates a backup of files before overwriting them
-d maintains symbolic and hard links during copying
-f forces a copy and overwrites existing files
-i asks for confirmation before overwriting an existing file
-l creates a hard link rather than a copy of a file
-P copies files into a target directory hierarchy (which is created if necessary)
-p also copies the permissions and modification times of the files
-r recursively copies subdirectories and their contents
-R see -r

-s	creates a symbolic link rather than a copy of a `file`
-S *suffix*	changes the extension for backup files to *suffix*
-u	prevents the overwriting of a file that has the same name and a newer date
-v	displays the name of each `file` on copying
-x	ignores directories on any file system different from the source file
-V {numbered, existing, simple}	determines the kind of version control:

numbered   always creates a numbered backup

existing   creates a numbered backup only for files for which such a backup already exists, and in all other cases creates a simple backup

simple   always creates a simple backup

---

cpio `options [arguments]`

cpio

Copies files into an archive, displays the contents of an archive, or extracts files from an archive. The archives can be on magnetic tape, hard disk, or floppy disks. `cpio` has three modes of operation, selected by the options `-i` (*copy in* = unpack), `-o` (*copy out* = pack), and `-p` (*copy pass* = copy from directories). `cpio` was designed to work with the `find` command.

Available options

-0	accepts file names terminated with null instead of newline (copy out and copy pass modes)
-a	resets the access times of files that are read so that the reading cannot be discerned from the file date
-A	adds files to an existing archive (with options `-O` or `-F`)
-b	during extraction (copy in), exchanges words and half-words (little/big endian)
-B	increases the input/output buffer from 512 to 5120 bytes
-c	uses the (old) portable ASCII format for the file headers
-C *n*	sets the input/output buffer to *n* bytes
-d	automatically creates the necessary subdirectories during extraction

-E *file*   extracts the files whose names are in *file* (copy in)

-f   copies only the files that do not match the specified search pattern

-F *file*   uses the specified *file* as an archive instead of the standard output device. *file* can also contain the name of a host in order to write the archive to a remote magnetic tape (`-F zeus:/dev/tape`)

-H *format*   reads/writes header information in the specified *format*:

bin	old binary format
odc	old portable format (POSIX.1)
newc	new portable format (SVR4)
crc	new SVR4 format with CRC checksums
tar	old tar-compatible format
ustar	POSIX.1-compatible tar format
hpbin	old HP UNIX binary format
hpodc	portable HP UNIX format

-i   puts `cpio` in copy-in mode (extraction of an archive)

-I *file*   uses the specified file instead of the standard input device. A host name (`zeus:/dev/tape`) can be specified, for example, to access an archive on a remote magnetic tape drive

-L   dereferences symbolic links, meaning that not the link but the file to which the link refers is copied

-m   the original modification date of a file is retained on creation of a new file

-M *msg*   enables multivolume archives. If a storage medium is full, the message `msg` is displayed on the screen. The variable `%d` can be used within the message to display the current number of the medium

-n   on display of the directory listing, the UID and GID are displayed as numeric values

-o   puts `cpio` in copy-out mode (creation of an archive)

-O *file*   uses the specified file instead of the standard output device. A machine name (`zeus:/dev/tape`) can be specified, for example, to access an archive on a remote magnetic tape drive

-p   puts `cpio` in copy-pass mode (copy directories locally)

173

-R [user][;.][group]   changes the file owner in copy-out and copy-pass modes and can only be used by the administrator

-s   exchange bytes in copy-in mode

-S   exchange halfwords in copy-in mode

-t   displays a list of the contents of an archive

-u   permits overwriting of files with the same name and an older version

-v   displays a list of file names. A verbose version can be obtained by combining with the option `-t`.

-V   displays a period (".") for each processed file

Examples

```
find. -name ''*.txt'' -print — cpio -ocv > /dev/tape
```
        backs up all files that end with "txt" into an archive on magnetic tape

```
cpio -icdv < /dev/tape
```
        extracts all files from magnetic tape to the hard disk

```
find. -print — cpio -pdv /tmp
```
        copies all files from the current directory to `/tmp`

---

crontab `[-u user] file`
crontab `[-u user] operations`

crontab

Replaces, edits, lists, or deletes a user's `crontab` file. The administrator can process any user's `crontab` file by using the option `-u`.

Available operations

-e   edits the `crontab` file in the default editor (environment variable `EDITOR`)

-l   lists a user's `crontab` file

-r   deletes the `crontab` file

---

csh `[options] [arguments]`

csh

Command interpreter with a syntax based on C.

csplit [options] file [expression]

Splits the specified file into multiple smaller files and displays the sizes of the generated files. If the specified file name is "-," then data are read from the standard input device. The locations for the splitting can be specified by an optional expression of the following form:

number specifies the number of lines after which a new output file is to be created

/regexp/[offset] regular expression that specifies the splitting locations; an optional positive (+) or negative (-) line offset can be defined

%regexp%[offset] like the above expression, but in this case the specified section is skipped rather than written to a file

{repetitions} induces the repeated application of an expression to which it is appended. If an asterisk (*) is specified instead of a number, then the expression is applied until the end of the input file is reached

Available options

-f *prefix* specifies the prefix for the generated output files

-b *suffix* changes the suffix of the generated files. The format of suffix is based on the format commands of printf. %d sets the number of the output file in decimal form, while %x results in hexadecimal representation

-k already generated files are preserved, even if the command is aborted

-n *n* length of the sequential number in the name of the output files (default 2)

-q suppresses screen output

-s see -q

-z suppresses the generation of files of length 0

Examples

csplit -k linux.txt '%cut%' {30}

splits the file linux.txt at positions "cut" into at most 30 output files

175

```
csplit -k list.txt 10 {100}
```
splits the file `list.txt` into at most 100 files with 10 lines each

---

ctags [options] files

Reads the specified C, Fortran, Pascal, LaTeX, or Lisp source files and generates a list of functions and macros defined therein. This list can be processed in the `vi` or `emacs` editor. A keyword list (tag file) is generated with the name `tags` in the current directory.

Available options

-a	appends the names found to an existing list
-B	generates a search pattern for a backwards search in `vi`
-C	activates C++ mode, where `.c` and `.h` files are treated as C++ code
-d	generates entries for preprocessor definitions as well
-f *file*	writes the names it finds to `file`. If `-f` is not specified, then the file `tags` is used
-F	generates a search pattern for forward search in `vi` (default)
-H	displays a help text
-i *file*	continues the search for a tag in the specified *file*
-o *file*	changes the name of the output *file*
-S	ignores indents
-t	also generates a tag for type definitions
-T	also generates a tag for type definitions, structures, enumerations, and C++ member functions
-u	the tag list is updated
-v	generates an index file in `vgrind` format and outputs it to the standard output device
-V	displays the version number
-w	suppresses warnings about duplicate entries
-x	generates a cross reference list in `cxref` format and outputs it to the standard output device

cut options [files]

Cuts a series of fields or columns from a line of the input file. One of the options `-b`, `-c` or `-f` must be specified. Each of these options expects a list that can contain numbers separated by commas or fields defined by hyphens.

Available options

-b *list*   selects the character at the position defined in *list*

-c *list*   selects the columns specified in *list*

-d *c*   is output together with `-f` to specify the field delimiter character (*c*)

-f *list*   selects the fields (separated by tabulators or the delimiting character) from *list*

-s   restricts output to lines that contain the field separator

Example

cut `-d: -f1,3` /etc/passwd
          outputs the login names and user IDs of all users

date [options] [+format]
date [options] [string]

In the former form, the current date and time are returned in a `format` that can be provided optionally. With the second form, the system administrator can set the system time.

Output format

%%	percent sign
%n	new line
%t	tabulator
%H	hour (00 .. 23)
%I	hour (01–12)
%k	hour (0 .. 23)
%l	hour (1 .. 12)
%M	minute (00 .. 59)

%p	AM or PM
%r	time in 12-hour format (hh:mm:ss[AM|PM])
%s	seconds since January 1, 1970, 0:00
%S	seconds (00 .. 59)
%T	time in 24-hour format
%X	time in local format
%Z	time zone, if defined, else empty
%a	local abbreviation of day name
%A	local name of day of week
%b	local abbreviation of month name (Jan ... Dec)
%B	local month name (January ... December)
%c	local date with time and time zone
%d	day of month (01 .. 31)
%D	date (mm/dd/yy)
%h	identical to %b
%j	sequential day of the year (001 .. 366)
%m	month as number (01 .. 12)
%U	week as number (0053) where Sunday is the first day
%w	day of week as number (0 .. 6)
%W	week as number (00 .. 53) where Monday is the first day
%x	local representation of the date (dd/mm/yy)
%y	last two digits of the year (00 .. 99)
%Y	year (1995 ...)

Format of the string to set the time

DD	day of month
hh	hour
mm	minute
CC	first two digits of year (=century)
YY	last two digits of year
ss	seconds

Available options

-d *date*   outputs the specified date (which can contain the month name, time zone, ... etc.)

-s *date*   sets the date in arbitrary format (which can contain the month name, time zone, ... etc.)

-u   ignores time zone and uses UTC (Universal Coordinated Time)

---

dd [options=value ...]

copies from the standard input device or a specified file to the standard output device or another specified file. The most frequent options are `if` to specify the input file and `of` to specify the output file. dd, for example, can be used to write a kernel image file directly onto a diskette or to make a boot diskette from a disk image.

Available options

bs=n   sets the block size for input and output to `n` bytes. Optionally, `n` can be specified with units, e.g., 8k for 8 kilobytes

cbs=n   determines the size of a field in converting to bytes

conv=flags   converts the input according to the following arguments:

    ascii   EBCDIC to ASCII conversion

    ebcdic   ASCII to EBCDIC conversion

    ibm   ASCII to IBM EBCDIC conversion

    block   converts variable-length fields to fields of length `cbs` and fills the spaces with blanks

    unblock   converts fixed-length fields (`cbs`) to variable-length fields

    lcase   converts uppercase to lowercase letters

    ucase   converts lowercase to uppercase letters

    swap   swaps every two bytes of the input file

    noerror   ignores errors during reading

    notrunc   does not truncate the output file

    sync   fills spaces in the input blocks of size `ibs` with zeros

count=n copies only `n` blocks

if=file specifies the input `file`

of=file specifies the output `file`

ibs=n   sets the size of the input buffer

obs=n   sets the size of the output buffer

skip=n   skips n blocks of input

---

df [options] [paths]

Outputs the number of occupied and free blocks of file system. If no path is specified, then a list of all current file systems is output. If a path is specified, an overview is provided of the associated file systems. Alternatively, the direct path of a device (/dev/hda1) on which the file system is located can be specified. Normally only real file systems with a storage volume greater than zero are output.

Available options

-a   displays all current file systems, including those of size zero
-i   instead of block information, displays i-node statistics
-k   uses a block size of one kilobyte (default)
-P   uses POSIX output format
-t *type*   restricts output to file systems of a certain type
-x *Type*   ignores file systems of a certain type during output

---

diff [options] file1 file2

Compares two files or all files in two directories. If one of the two paths is specified as "-", then the files are expected from the standard input device. The output of diff lists all lines that occur in only one file or that are different. This output can be used by patch to make changes in files. Another alternative for comparing or merging files is the Emacs Lisp program ediff.

Available options

-a   treats all input files as text files and compares linewise
-b   ignores differences in the number of blanks (at the end of a line as well)
-B   ignores blank lines
-c   generates output with three lines of context around each difference
-C *n*   like -c, but *n* lines of context are output around each difference

-d   uses a better, although slower, algorithm for file comparison

-D *name*   mixes the two files and inserts appropriate preprocessor instructions (`#ifdef` *name*) to make the two versions distinguishable. If *name* is defined during compilation, then the version is output to `file1`, otherwise to `file2`

-e   outputs instructions for the `ed` editor to be able to generate `file2` from `file1`

-f   like option `-e`, but reversed, yet it cannot be used as an `ed` script

-h   is ignored

-H   uses heuristics to increase the speed

-i   ignores differences in upper/lower case

-l   (only when comparing whole directories) the output can be processed with the command `pr` so that each file begins on a new page

-n   generates output in RCS format

-N   in comparing two directories, missing files are considered as existing, but empty

-q   simply reports whether the files are different

-r   (only when comparing whole directories) subdirectories are handled recursively and all files are compared

-s   reports whether two files are identical

-S *file*   starts comparing directories with a certain file

-t   replaces tabs with blanks

-T   outputs a tab instead of a blank at the start of every output line

-u   generates output in GNU-specific "unified" format

-v   displays the version number

-w   ignores blanks and tabs when comparing lines

-x *pattern*   ignores files and subdirectories that match the specified *pattern* (when comparing whole directories)

-y   outputs in easy-to-read, two-column format

`diff3` [options] file1 file2 file3

Compares three files linewise.

diff3

Available options

-a	linewise comparison treating all input files as text files
-A	inserts all changes between `file2` and `file3` in `file1` and marks conflicts
-e	generates a script for the `ed` editor that integrate all changes from `file2` to `file3` in `file1`
-E	like option `-e`, but the output is less verbose
-i	generates `w` and `q` commands at the end of a generated `ed` script
-m	applies the edit script to `file1` and displays it
-T	outputs a tab instead of a blank at the start of every output line
-v	outputs the version number of the command
-x	like option `-e`, but only overlapping changes are output
-X	like option `-E`, but only overlapping changes are output
-3	like option `-e`, but only nonoverlapping changes are output

---

dirname `pathname`

dirname

Extracts the directory part of a complete path specification (counterpart to `basename`). If the path does not contain a file at the end, then "." is returned.

---

du `[options] [files - directories]`

du

Outputs the sizes of the specified files or directories.

Available options

-a	outputs the sizes of all files, not just directories
-b	outputs the file size in bytes
-k	outputs the file size in kilobytes
-l	outputs the sizes of (hard) linked files, even if this means handling them doubly
-s	outputs the total size of all files and subdirectories
-x	ignores directories in different file systems

echo [-n] [text]

This command is usually built into shells. It outputs text to the standard output device. The option -n suppresses the output of the newline character.

ed [options] [file]

This is an antiquated standard editor which, apart from its use with the diff command, is no longer of any importance.

egrep

See grep.

env [options] [variable=value] [command]

If invoked without parameters, this command produces a list of all environment variables. In addition, this command permits starting commands in a modified environment. In the command line, new variables can be defined or existing ones removed.

Available options

-i   ignores the inherited environment
-u *name*   removes the specified environment variable

expr arg1 operator arg2 [operator arg3 ...]

Evaluates an expression and outputs the result to the standard output device. Expressions can be numeric, logical, or relational. This command is usually used in shell scripts.

Arithmetic operators

+, -, *, /, % (modular rest)

Relational operators

=, !=, >, >=, <, <=

Logical operators

> − (or), & (and),
>
> : (seek Arg2 as a regular expression in Arg1)

Examples

`expr 7+8/2`

> evaluates to 7 (integer arithmetic, left to right!)

`expr $s="hello"`

> evaluates to 1 if s contains the string "hello," else 0

---

false

This command does nothing and returns *false* (not 0). (Also see `true`.)

---

fdformat [-n] device

Executes low-level formatting of a diskette. The required parameter is the path of the corresponding `device`. The first drive is addressed as `/dev/fd0XXX`; the second, as `/dev/fd1XXX`. The -n option suppresses subsequent verification of the diskette.

Device	Sectors	Tracks	Size	Capacity (KB)
/dev/fd0h1200	15	80	5 ¼	1200
/dev/fd0d720	9	80	3 ½	720
/dev/fd0h1440	18	80	3 ½	1440

---

fgrep

See grep

---

file [options] files

Outputs the types of specified `files`. The file type is recognized on the basis of an extensible rule file (`/etc/magic/etc/magic`).

Available options

-c   for checking the rule file

-f *file*   examines the files listed in *file*

-m *file*   uses the specified rule *file* instead of /etc/magic

-L   also follows symbolic links

-z   enables the processing of compressed files

---

find pathname constraints

This command recursively searches in directories for files that meet all the specified constraints. The list of constraints is evaluated from left to right. Individual constraints can be negated by a preceding exclamation mark (!). An OR conjunction between two expression is defined with -o. find is particularly useful in combination with other commands (e.g., cpio).

Numeric specifications can be represented in three ways

        +n   value larger than n

        n   value equal to n

        -n   value smaller than n

Available options (always true)

-depth files contained in a directory are processed before the directory itself

-follow also branches to directories indicated by symbolic links (follows symbolic links)

Possible constraints

-amin *n* files accessed in the last *n* minutes

-anewer *file* files accessed more recently than the specified *file*

-atime *n* files that were last accessed *n* days ago

-ctime *n* files that were last modified (either the file itself, the permissions or the owner) *n* days ago

-fstype *type* files in a certain *type* of file system (e.g., ext2, msdos, proc)

-group *group* files belonging to a certain *group* (name or ID)

-inum *n*   files with i-node number *n*

-links *n*   files that possess *n* links

-local   files physically stored on the local system

-mtime *n*   files that were last modified (only the file itself) *n* days ago

-name *pattern*   the names of the files match the specified wildcard *pattern*

-newer *file*   the last modification of the files must be more recent than the specified *file* (see also mtime)

-nogroup   files whose group does not exist in /etc/groups

-nouser   files whose owner does not exist in /etc/passwd

-perm *nnn*   the permissions of the files must match the octal representation *nnn*

-size *n* [*c, k*]   files of size *n* blocks, *n* bytes, or *n* kilobytes

-type *c*   files of type *c*, where *c* must derive from the following list:

b	block special file
c	character special file
d	directory
p	FIFO or named pipe
l	symbolic link
f	normal file

-user *user*   files belonging to a certain *user* (name or ID)

Possible actions

-exec *command* {}\;   executes the *command* for each file and tests whether the return code is 0. During execution, {} is replaced by the name of the current file

-ok *command* {}\;   like exec, but the user must confirm the *commands* with "y"

-print   outputs files or directories found

-printf *format*   like -print, but the format of the output can be influenced by a *format* string

Examples

```
find. -typef -print
```
    outputs all normal files in the current directory and its subdirectories

```
find ./usr/include -typef\ -execgrep "read" {}\;-print
```
        searches all normal files in `/usr/include` for the character string "read"

---

finger [options] [user]

Provides information on users. `user` can be in the form of `name`, `name@host` or `@host`. In the first two forms the names of the users, the times, the last logins, and additional information are output. If the file `.plan` or `.project` exists in the `user`'s home directory, then it is also displayed. If only one host is specified with `@host`, then all users are listed who are currently logged into that system.

Available options

-l   forces verbose output (at `@host`)

-m   the specified `user` must exactly match the user name. Without this option the specified name is also compared with the full name of the user as stored in the file `/etc/passwd`

-p   the files `.plan` and `.project` of the respective `user` are not displayed

-s   forces brief output format

---

ftp [options] [host]

This program is for transferring files with the ftp protocol. The `host` can be specified by name or IP address. If no `host` is specified, then the program responds with a prompt that allows entry of ftp commands. Entering `help` evokes a help text.

Available options

-d   debug mode

-g   toggles off the use of wildcards for file names

-i   turns off queries (`mget`, `mput`)

-n   suppresses automatic login on computer listed in the file `.netrc`

-v   displays all the ftp server's messages

---

gcc [options] [files]

gcc

In addition to C, C++, and Objective C, the GNU C compiler supports back ends for other languages such as Ada and Pascal. A more detailed description of these features can be found in the GNU Info documents.

---

grep [options] regexp [files]

grep

Searches files or data from the standard input device linewise for a regular expression (regexp) and outputs the found lines to the standard output device.

Available options

-b	additionally outputs the byte position where the expression was found
-c	outputs only the number of lines in which the expression was found
-h	suppresses the output of file names
-i	ignores differences in size and (upper/lower) case
-l	outputs only the names, but not the lines, of files in which the expression was found
-n	outputs the line numbers of found lines
-s	suppresses error messages in case a file does not exist or cannot be opened
-v	searches for lines that do not contain the regular expression

---

groff [options] [files]

groff

groff is the GNU variant of nroff and troff. The command serves to format Manual pages and other documents that are available in the appropriate format. Additional preprocessors such as eqn or tbl are integrated in groff and can be activated with options. The results can be stored in ASCII, DVI or PostScript format. In formatting documents, it is important to specify the macro package used. For Manual pages, for example, the option -man would be specified. The formatted file is written to the standard output device.

Available options

-a	outputs pure ASCII format
-e	activates the eqn preprocessor
-E	suppresses error messages
-h	outputs help text
-m *macro*	uses a special *macro* package for formatting
	-man macros for Manual pages
	-ms ms macro package
-p	activates pic preprocessor
-s	activates soelim preprocessor
-t	activates tbl preprocessor
-T *format*	specifies output *format* (ascii, ps, dvi) an
-v	outputs the version number

Example

zeus:/home/uhl> **groff -man -Tps ls.1 > ls.ps**

formats the Manual page ls.1 with the corresponding macro package and outputs the result in PostScript format to the file ls.ps

---

groups [user]

Outputs the groups to which the specified user belongs. A parameterless invocation lists all the current user's own groups, and with a parameter the groups of the specified user. The command evaluates the files /etc/passwd and /etc/groups.

groups

---

gzip [options] [files]

Compresses or decompresses files using the LZ77 method and adds the extension ".gz" to the file name. If no file (or "-") is specified, then the standard input device is read and output goes to the standard output device. gzip can also decompress files packed with compress (ending in ".Z").

gzip

Available options

-a   adapts the end of line in ASCII texts to the respective system (CRLF or LF)

-c   writes the results to the standard output device without overwriting the input file

-d   decompresses packed files

-f   forces an overwrite of existing files

-l   for a compressed file, displays its size in packed and unpacked form, the compression rate, and the name of the original file

-q   suppresses warnings

-r   recursively works through subdirectories

-S *.suffix*   changes the file *suffix* for compressed files

-v   displays the name and the compression rate for each file

-#   sets the quality of compression from 1 (poor) to 9 (good), where default compression is 6

---

head [options] [files]

head

Displays the first 10 lines of the specified (text) files. On specification of multiple files, the file name precedes the file contents in the output.

Available options

-#   changes the number of lines to be output to the specified value

-c *n*[*b*|*k*|*m*]   outputs the first *n* bytes, where the specification can be made in bytes (*b*), kilobytes (*k*), or megabytes (*m*)

-q   suppresses the output of file name

---

hostname [name]

hostname

Parameterless invocation displays the name of the host; otherwise the specified name is set. The host name is usually set on system startup and requires superuser permissions.

id [options]

Displays the real and effective user ID (UID) and all groups (GID) of the current user.

Available options

-g   displays only GID
-G   displays only the additional groups to which a user belongs
-n   displays GID or UID as name (only in combination with options -g, -u, -G)
-r   displays the real instead of the effective GID (only in combination with options -g, -u, -G)
-u   displays only UID

join [options] file1 file2

Joins two alphabetically sorted ASCII files via a key. Lines with identical keys are joined and written to the standard output device. Keys must be separated by blanks or tabs. If no further options are specified, the first column is used as the key.

Available options

-a [n]   adds an empty line to the output if one line of file n (1 or 2) does not have a matching key in the other file
-e *string*   replaces empty output fields with the specified character *string*
-j n m   uses column m of file n (1 or 2) as the key
-o $n.m$ displays only column m of file n
-t z   uses character z as field delimiter (input/output)

kill [options] processes

This command is usually built into a shell. It sends a signal to one or more processes. Without further options, a TERM signal is sent, which orders a process to terminate. Only the system administrator can send signals to processes that she/he does not own. The processes are specified with their process number (PID). The signals can be specified numerically or symbolically.

Available options

-l   lists all signal names

-signal sends a certain *signal* to the specified `processes`. The following signals are useful in this context:

No.	Name	Explanation
1	SIGHUP	Generated on interruption of a terminal connection. For many daemons it serves to read the configuration files anew
2	SIGINT	Equivalent to entering <Ctrl-c>
3	SIGQUIT	Terminates a process and invokes a core dump
9	SIGKILL	Terminates a process. This signal cannot be intercepted
15	SIGTERM	Terminates a process (default).
10	SIGUSR1	User-specific signal whose meaning is different in each application
12	SIGUSR2	See SIGUSR1

ksh [options] [arguments]

ksh

See bash.

last [options] [attribute]

last

Provides information from the login statistics (`/etc/wtmp`). Without additional arguments, it outputs a list of all login, logout, shutdown, and reboot activities. This list contains the name of the user or the event, the login terminal, the login host, and the time. A selection can be limited to certain entries by specifying search attributes (name, login terminal).

Available options

-#   limits output to a certain number of lines

-f *file*   uses the specified *file* instead of `/etc/wtmp` as the data base

-t *terminal*   lists only logins entered from a particular *terminal*

-h *computer*   lists only logins entered from a certain *computer*

Example

```
hermes:/root# last uhl
uhl    ttyp4    mobby      Sun Jan 29 17:24    still logged in
uhl    ttyp2    tonne      Sun Jan 29 16:32 - 16:47 (00:15)

wtmp begins Sun Jan 29 15:18
hermes:/root#
```

ld [options] object_files

The linker links individual `object files` to an executable program. It is seldom invoked directly. Normally the C compiler or the `make` command automatically invokes the linker.

ld

ldd [options] [programs]

Lists the dynamic libraries that a `program` needs.

ldd

Available options

-d   carries out a relocation and lists missing functions (only ELF format)

-r   carries out a relocation for data and program code and lists missing objects (only ELF format)

-v   outputs the version number of the command

-V   outputs the version number of the dynamic linker (ld.so)

lex [options] [files]

The scanner generator creates the output file `lex.yy.c` from a scanner grammar as input file.

lex

`ln` [options] path target_path

Creates a link. Without options, it creates a hard link to a file. With the option `-s` a symbolic link is created that could also point to a directory. If `target path` already exists and is a file, then an error message is output. Only with the option `-f` is this file overwritten. If `target_path` is a directory, then the links are created in this directory.

Available options

-f   any existing files are overwritten without confirmation
-s   symbolic links are created

`lpc` [command [argument]]

Serves to control printer spoolers. It enables the activation and deactivation of individual printers and their printing queues, shifting printer jobs within the printing queues, and outputting status information. Invoking `lpc` without an argument produces an interactive command modus. Alternatively, these commands can also passed to `lpc` on invocation.

Available commands

help   displays a list of available commands
abort {*all* | *printer*}   terminates active spooler(s) and disables the corresponding *printer*(s)
clean {*all* | *printer*}   removes all incomplete files from the specified *printer* queue(s)
disable {*all* | *printer*}   disables the corresponding *printer*(s)
down {*all* | *printer*} *message*   turns off the specified queue, disables *printer*(s) and writes the specified *message* in the printer status file. This message is output on invocation of `lpq`.
enable {*all* | *printer*}   enables the specified printer queue(s) and permits the addition of new jobs
exit, quit   ends the `lpc` program

restart {*all* | *printer*}   attempts to restart *printer* daemon(s)

start {*all* | *printer*}   activates *printer*(s) and starts *printer* daemon(s) for the specified *printer*(s)

status {*all* | *printer*}   outputs status information on currently active *printer* daemon(s) and queue(s)

stop {*all* | *printer*}   stops the *printer* daemon on completion of the current job and disables the *printer*

topq *printer* [*job#*] [*user*]   places the specified job at the head of the queue

up {*all* | *printer*}   activates queue(s) and starts *printer* daemon(s)

---

lpq [options] [job#s] [user]

Provides information on the current status of printer queues.

Available options

-l   verbose status report on each job
-P *name*   selects a printer queue

---

lpr [options] [files]

Sends `files` to a printer queue. Alternatively, data can be printed via the standard input device. Invocation without options outputs to the queue `lp`.

Available options

-# *n*   creates *n* copies of the specified documents
-C *text*   prints a job classification on the title page
-h   suppresses the output of a header before a print job
-J *job*   prints a *job* name on the title page
-m   sends a mail to the user on completion of the job
-P *name*   selects the specified printer queue
-r   deletes the file after printing (with option -s)
-s   file is not spooled but linked. Thus the printer file must not be deleted during printing.
-U *user*   prints the *user* name on the title page

lprm [options] [job#s] [user]

Removes entries from a printer queue. *Job numbers* or *user* names can be specified as selection criteria. If no argument is specified, the active job is removed.

Available options

-          removes all entries from a queue
-P name   selects the specified printer queue

---

ls [options] [files]

Displays the contents of directories or lists specific files. If no files are specified, the contents of the current directory are listed. If files are specified, then only the such files are listed that match the file name (with wildcards).

Available options

-a	displays all files, including those beginning with a period
-A	like option - a, but suppresses the entries " . " and " . . "
-B	ignores backup files that end in tilde (~)
-b	displays nonprintable characters as octal numbers
-c	sorts files by time of last status change
-C	displays only file names, but in multiple columns (default)
-d	on specification of a directory name, lists only the directory itself, not its contents
-f	unsorted output
-F	appends a special character to each file name to indicate the file's type (normal file, directory, executable file, link, . . .)
-G	suppresses the output of group in long format
-i	displays the associated node for each file
-k	displays file size in kilobytes
-l	long format displays every file in a line along with its permissions, owner, group, size, etc.
-L	for symbolic links, shows the file or directory to which the link points rather than the link itself

-m	lists file names linewise, separated by commas
-n	lists UID and GID numerically
-r	lists `files` sorted backward
-R	recursively lists subdirectories and their contents
-s	lists file size in kilobytes before the file name
-S	sorts list by file size
-t	sorts list by date of last modification, with newer files coming first
-u	sorts list by time of last access
-x	lists `files` in horizontally sorted columns
-X	lists `files` sorted by file extension

`m4` [options] [files]

This macro processor is used for various program files, in the GNU Autoconf system, and for `fvwm` configuration files. The language is described in the GNU Info system.

m4

`mail` [options] [addresses]

This program is for reading and sending e-mail. Users should instead use the program `pine` or a graphical mail reader. However, `mail` proves superb for simply sending text files because the contents can be transferred via the standard input device.

mail

Example

`maillinux@fh-heilbronn.de < critique.txt`

`make` [options] [targets]

Reads a makefile and updates one or more `targets`. `make` is usually used for compiling of source files. It is described in detail in the GNU Info system.

make

Available options

-C *directory*   changes to the specified sub*directory* before a makefile is read

-d   provides additional debugging information

-e   environment variables overwrite corresponding variables in the makefile

-f *makefile*   uses the specified *makefile*

-I *directory*   searches in the specified *directory* for imported makefiles

-k   on error, aborts only the current `target`, not the complete make process

-n   only outputs commands without executing them

-p   outputs internal macro definitions

-r   uses no default rules

-s   suppresses screen output

-t   provides `files` to be processed with the current date without executing the corresponding operation

-w   displays the current working directory before and after executing an operation

---

man [options] [[section] name]

man

Displays On-line Manual pages pagewise on the screen. These pages are located in a subdirectory under /usr/man or in other directories listed in the environment variable MANPATH.

Available options

-a   displays all Manual pages that match the specified name

-f   equivalent to the command `whatis`

-h   displays a help page

-k   equivalent to the command `apropos`

-M *path*   specifies a list of additional directories in which to search for Manual pages (see MANPATH)

-w   displays not the contents but the access path of a Manual page

mesg [y − n]

Determines whether other users can write messages on the terminal with write. If mesg is invoked without options, the current status is displayed.

mkdir [options] directories

Creates directories.

Available options

-m *perms*   creates a new directory with the specified *perm*issions
-p   if a directory path is specified where individual subdirectories do not exist, then these are created also

more [options] [files]

Displays files by (screen) page. **Enter** scrolls one line down and the space bar advances to the next screen page. **h** displays help with all commands and **q** quits the more command. If no file is specified, then more reads from the standard input device.

Available options

+#   begins with the specified line number
-d   displays the message "Press space to continue, 'q' to quit" at the end of a screen page
-f   counts logical rather than screen lines for page breaks and counts broken lines only once
-l   ignores form-feed control character (^{L})
-s   suppresses the output of multiple neighboring blanks
-u   suppresses underlining

mtools

This is a group of commands that permit simple access to MS-DOS file systems. Normally these are used to handle diskettes. Note that access to a DOS partition of a hard disk is simpler if it is mounted (see mount.). The individual commands largely correspond to the DOS commands. This means that floppy disk drives can be accessed with DOS's usual letter designations (A:, B:) if the drives were correctly configured in the file /etc/mtools.

Commands

mattrib   modifies file attributes
mcd   changes the current directory
mcopy   copies files
mdel   deletes files
mdir   displays a directory listing
mformat   formats a low-level formatted diskette with a DOS file system
mlabel   changes the volume label
mmd   creates a subdirectory
mrd   removes a subdirectory
mren   renames a file
mtype   displays the contents of a file

---

mount [options] [device] [mount_location]

mount

Links new file systems into the directory tree. A file system is attached to the UNIX file tree at a defined mount location. Unspecified parameters are taken from the entries of the file /etc/fstab.

Available options

-a   automatically mounts all file systems specified in /etc/fstab
-f   suppresses the actual mount system invocation (practical with option -v)
-n   suppresses entries in /etc/mtab
-o *opts*   additional *opt*ions that depend on the respective file system

General options

async   all input and output is asynchronous
auto   the file system can be mounted with the -a option

defaults standard options: `rw`, `suid`, `dev`, `exec`, `auto`, `nouser`, `async`

dev permits the use of character- and block-oriented devices

exec permits execution of commands

noauto can only be mounted explicitly, but not with the option `-a`,

nodev suppresses the use of character- and block-oriented devices

noexec suppresses the execution of commands

nosuid SUID and SGID bits have no effect

nouser forbids a normal user to mount file systems

remount permits remounting of a file systems, e.g., to change mount options

ro mounts the file system as read-only. This option must be specified to mount CD-ROM file systems.

rw mounts the file system for reading and writing

suid enables the execution of SUID and SGID commands

sync all input and output operations are synchronous

user permits a normal user to mount the file system

File-system–specific options

case={*lower | asis*} (hpfs) sets (upper/lower) case sensitivity

check=*value* (ext2) enables the choice of consistency checks before mounting a file systems

  none no consistency checks

  normal check i-node and block bitmap (default)

  strict also checks consistency of free blocks

check=*value* (msdos) determines the form for specifying file names

  relaxed case insensitive, long file names truncated

  normal special characters (`*`, `?`, `<`, ...) not accepted (default)

  strict no long file names and no special characters

conv=*value* determines whether end-of-line (EOL) character is converted on access to file system (msdos, hpfs, iso9660)

  binary no EOL conversion (default)

  text CRLF/LF conversion for all files

  auto no conversion on files with the following extensions: `exe`, `com`, `bin`, `app`, `sys`, `drv`, `ovl`,

ovr, obj, lib, dll, pif, arc, zip, lha, zoo,
lai, z, arj, tz, taz, tzp, tpz, gif, bmp,
tif, gl, jpg, pcx, tfm, vf, gf, pk, pxl, dvi

block=*value*   specifies block size for iso9660 file systems

cruft   sets the *cruft* flag to overcome an error in certain CD-ROM premastering programs (iso9660)

debug   creates debug messages (ext2, msdos)

errors=*value*   determines error handling (ext2)

> **continue**   no special error handling (default)
>
> **remount ro**   file system is remounted as read-only
>
> **panic**   on error, force a kernel panic

fat=*value*   overwrites the automatically detected *value* for the FAT type (available values being 12 and 16) (msdos)

gid=*value*   establishes the GID for each file of the file system (msdos, hpfs)

grpid   new files receive the same GID as the directory in which they are created (ext2)

nocheck   equivalent to check=none (ext2)

nogrpid   new files receive the GID of the creating process, as in System V (ext2, default)

norock   turns off Rockridge extensions, ending case sensitivity and long file names (iso9660)

quiet   suppresses corresponding error messages on attempts to execute the commands chmod and chown (msdos)

sb=*value*   uses an alternative superblock at the specified block position (normally at positions 1, 8193, 16385, ...) (ext2)

sysvgroups   see nogrpid

uid=*value*   determines the GID for each file in the file system (msdos, hpfs)

umask=*value*   determines the umask for files (msdos, hpfs) 1

-r   file system is mounted as read-only

-t *type*   mounts a file system of a certain *type* (default: minix; possible values: minix, ext, etx2, xiafs, msdos, hpfs, proc, nfs, iso9660, sysv, xenix, coherent)

-v   outputs verbose messages

mv [options] path target

Moves files and directories or renames them. If the target already exists and it is a file, it is overwritten; if it is a directory, the specified files and directories are moved into the existing directory. If the target does not exist, then only a file or a directory can be specified as the source, and it is renamed to the target name.

Available options

- **-b**   creates a backup of a file before overwriting it
- **-f**   does not ask for confirmation before overwriting files
- **-i**   asks for confirmation before overwriting files
- **-u**   moves a file only if it is newer than a target file of the same name
- **-S**   see cp command
- **-V**   see cp command

mv

---

nice [-n value − -value] commands [arguments]

Executes commands with a higher nice-level, i.e., a lower priority. nice is usually integrated in the shell. The maximum nice-level is 19. The system administrator can also specify negative values to -20. A default nice-level of 10 is used in lieu of a specification.

nice

---

nm [options] files

Outputs the symbol table of object files or libraries.

nm

---

nohup command [arguments] &

This command is usually integrated into the shell. It prevents termination of the specified command when the shell terminates.

nohup

---

nroff [options] files

Formats files that contain corresponding format statements for output on the screen or the printer (see also groff).

nroff

openwin

openwin

Shell script to start the X11 environment.

passwd [user]

passwd

Changes the user's own password. The system administrator can also change the passwords of other users.

pr [options] [files]

pr

Prepares text files for printing. The file contents are prepared pagewise and provided with a title line containing the date, the file name, and the page number.

Available options

+page begins printing starting with the specified *page*
-column produces multiple-*column* output
-a prints columns alongside rather than under one another
-c outputs nonprintable characters in """ notation
-d double-spaced printout
-e[chars[width]] replaces any number of *characters* with a number of blanks. The default value for tab characters is 8 blanks.
-f produces a form feed at the end of a page instead of generating a series of blank lines
-h text replaces the file name in the title line with the specified *text*
-i[chars[width]] reverse effect of option -e
-l length determines the *length* of a page (default 66 lines)
-n[chars[width]] outputs a sequential number before each line; optionally, a *character* that separates the number from the text and the *width* of the number can be specified
-o width creates a left margin of specified *width*
-r suppresses error messages for files that cannot be opened
-t suppresses the header and footer
-v outputs nonprintable characters in format
-w specifies page width in characters (default 72)

-x displays the processes that are not assigned to a terminal

---

ps [options]

Outputs a list of currently active processes.

Available options

-a displays the processes of all users
-h suppresses the header line
-j outputs the process' group ID and session ID
-l verbose output format
-m provides an overview of storage allocation
-r lists only currently running processes
-s provides information on signal status
-u outputs the name of the process owner and the start time
-w suppresses the truncation of command lines for wide output

---

pwd

Outputs the complete path of the current directory

---

rcp [options] sources target

Copies files between computers. The sources and the target are in the form user@host:path, whereby user@ can be omitted, in which case the current user name is used. For local files only the path is specified.

Available options

-r recursively copies subdirectories and their contents
-p retains the file attributes (date, permissions) during copying

---

rlogin [options] host

Similar to telnet, this command provides a connection to the specified host and logs in there. If the current user is entered on the remote host in the files .rhosts or /etc/hosts.equiv, then no password is required.

Available options

-l *name*   uses *name* as the user name on the remote host

---

rm [options] files

rm

Removes one or more files. Removing a file requires write permission in the containing directory. If the file is write protected, confirmation is required. Directories are removed with rmdir.

Available options

-f   removes files, even if write protected, without confirmation
-i   asks for confirmation for each file
-r   recursively removes subdirectories and their contents
-v   displays each file name on removal

---

rmdir [options] directories

rmdir

Removes subdirectories. A directory must be empty to be removed. Alternatively, rm can be used with option -r, which removes subdirectories and their contents.

---

rsh [options] host [commands]

rsh

Executes commands on a remote host. Access must be permitted via an entry in /etc/hosts.equiv or ~/.rhosts.

Available options

-l user   attempts to execute the specified command under another user name
-n   redirects the standard input device to /dev/null (works around problems with csh)

Example

```
rsh -luhl zeus.demo.de ls
```
> executes the command `ls` as user `uhl` on the host `zeus.demo.de`

---

sdiff `[options] file1 file2`

Compares two files and outputs the differences in two columns (also see `diff`). This output is easier to read than that of `diff`. Lines that are not contained in one of the two files are marked with "<" or ">." A pair of lines that differ are indicated with "|."

sdiff

---

sed `[options] [files]`

Modifies without interaction with the user. This command is usually used in shell scripts to replace, delete or insert text. If no `file` is specified, then `sed` works with the standard input device.

sed

Available options

-e '*statements*' executes the edit statements with the specified `files`

-f *script file* reads the edit statements from *script file*

-n suppresses the echo of input lines on the screen

---

shutdown `[options] time [message]`

Changes the run level of the system or terminates the system. A `time` and a warning `message` can be passed as arguments. For an immediate shutdown, the time `now` is specified.

shutdown

Available options

-c interrupts a shutdown in progress

-h halts the system with the termination of all processes and unmounts the file systems

-k does not execute a shutdown, but only displays the warning

-r reboots the system

-t *sec*   delay in seconds between the display of the warning message and sending the `kill signals`

---

sleep time

sleep

Sleeps the specified t ime in seconds. This command is usually used in shell scripts.

---

sort [options] [files]

sort

Sorts the lines in the specified f iles. If no f iles are specified, the standard input device is processed.

Available options

+*n-m*   sets the sorting key between fields *n* and *m*
-b   suppresses leading blanks
-c   checks whether the specified files are already sorted; if not, the program terminates with an error message
-d   ignores punctuation marks during sorting
-f   case-sensitive (upper/lower)
-i   ignores nonprintable ASCII characters
-m   mixes two input f iles
-M   interprets the first three characters as a month name (JAN, FEB, . . . , DEC) and sorts by month
-n   sorts numerically
-o *file*   redirects the standard output device to a file
-r   inverts sorting order
-t *char*   specifies the delimiting character for columns (default: blank or tab)
-u   removes duplicate lines

Example

```
sort +2n -t:/etc/passwd
```
          sorts the password file numerically according to the third column

strings [options] files

Searches for character strings in binary and object `files` or programs. A character string is considered to be any sequence of four or more printable characters terminated with null.

Available options

-a	normally for object files, only the code and data segments are searched; this option ensures that the whole file is processed
-f	each character string is preceded by the corresponding file name
-n	specifies the minimum length of the character string (default: 4)
-o	outputs the position of a character string in bytes

strip [options] files

Strips symbol, debug, line numbers, and other information from object `files` and programs, thus reducing their size.

stty [options] [modes]

Sets terminal IO `modes`. This includes all general settings of the terminal as well as speed and handshaking and the function of special characters. A list of all possible settings is displayed using the option `--help`.

Available options

-a	displays all current settings
–help	displays help text

su [-] [user] [arguments]

Starts a new shell as a different `user`. This program is used to log in on a terminal that is already being used by another user. Omitting

the `user` opens a root shell. The new shell is terminated by entering
exit or Ctrl + d . If "-" is specified as option, then the complete
login process is run on opening the new shell. In addition, the option
-c allows execution of commands under a different user ID.

---

tail [options] [files]

tail

Outputs the last 10 lines of the specified `files`.

Available options

-c[b|k|m] outputs the last *n* bytes in blocks (*b*), kilobytes (*k*), or
           megabytes (*m*)
-f   does not terminate after outputting the last lines, but waits
           until the `file` is written to. As soon as new lines are
           appended to the `file`, they are output. In this mode the
           program is terminated with break (Ctrl + c). This mode
           proves especially suitable for monitoring log files
-n   outputs the last n lines
-v   outputs the file name as title line

---

talk user [@host] [tty]

talk

Sets up a `talk` connection to the specified `user`. If this `user` is
logged in on multiple terminals, then the terminal to be used can be
entered in the command line. A `talk` connection splits the terminal
screen in two parts, with local input shown in the top half and remote
input in the lower half. The connection is terminated with Ctrl + c .
Unfortunately, there are two incompatible versions of `talk`, so that
connection to a different platform does not always succeed.

---

tar [options] [archive] [files]

tar

Manages tar archives (originally on magnetic tape). This command
writes files to an `archive` or reads them from an archive. At least
one of the following operations must be passed as parameter.

Available operations

-c	creates the `archive`
-r	appends files to an `archive` (not on tape)
-t	outputs the contents of an `archive`
-u	appends files to an `archive` if they are not already contained or if they have been modified (not on tape)
-x	extracts files from an `archive`

Additional options

-b *n*   sets the blocking factor to *n*

-f *archive*   specifies the *archive*, which can be a normal file or a device file such as `/dev/rmt0` for a tape drive or `/dev/fd0` for a diskette

-h   archives referenced files instead of their symbolic links

-k   prevents overwriting of existing files

-L   follows symbolic links

-m   sets the modification time on extracting `files` to the current time

-M   creates or extracts from a multivolume `archive`, which can encompass multiple diskettes or tapes

-N *date*   archives only `files` that are newer than the specified *date*

-o   sets the owner on extracting `files` to the current user

-O   extracts `files` to the standard output device

-v   displays the file name on archiving or extracting

-z   compresses the `archive` on creation and decompresses on extraction

Examples

`tar -cvf archive.tar *`

saves all files and subdirectories of the current directory in an archive named `archive.tar`

`tar -cvf /dev/fd0 *.txt`

saves all files in the current directory with the extension `.txt` from the diskette in the first floppy disk drive

`tar -xvfb20 /dev/rmt0`

extracts all files from the first tape drive (block size 20)

```
tar -tvf zarchive.tar.z
        lists the contents of a compressed tar archive
```

tee [options] [files]

This program is used as a filter. It copies the standard input device to the standard output device and the specified files.

Available options

-a   appends the data received from the standard input device to the end of the file instead of overwriting itself

-i   ignores interrupt signals

telnet [host [port]]

Opens a connection to the specified host using the telnet protocol. A port number can be specified optionally. This program is often used to test services that are available for connections on certain ports. If no host is specified, then telnet goes into command mode, where telnet commands can be entered. The command help lists all important commands.

test condition

Evaluates the specified condition and returns zero if the result is true, else a nonzero value. Alternatively, the condition can be put in square braces, which is primarily used in shell scripts.

Files

-b *file*   *file* is a block device
-c *file*   *file* is a character device
-d *file*   *file* is a directory
-f *file*   *file* is a normal file
-g *file*   set group ID bit (SGID) of *file* is set
-G *file*   effective GID matches owner's group
-k *file*   sticky bit of *file* is set
-O *file*   effective UID matches the file owner

p *file*   *file* is a named pipe
-r *file*   *file* exists and is readable
-s *file*   *file* is larger than 0 bytes
-S *file*   *file* is a socket
-t [n]   file descriptor *n* corresponds to a terminal
-u *file*   set user ID bit (SUID) of *file* is set
-w *file*   *file* exists and is writable
-x *file*   *file* exists and is executable
d1 **-ef** *d2*   files *d1* and *d2* are linked
d1 **-nt** *d2*   file *d1* is newer than *file d2*
d1 **-ot** *d2*   file *d1* is older than *file d2*

Character strings

-n *z1*   length of character string *z1* is greater than zero
-z *z1*   length of character string *z1* is zero
z1   character string *z1* is not null
z1=z2   *z1* is equal to *z2*
z1 != z2   *z1* is not equal to *z2*
z1< z2   *z1* is lexicographically smaller than *z2*
z1 > z2   *z1* is lexicographically greater than *z2*

Numeric conditions

n1 **-eq** *n2*   *n1* equals *n2*
n1 **-ge** *n2*   *n1* is greater than or equal to *n2*
n1 **-gt** *n2*   *n1* is greater than *n2*
n1 **-le** *n2*   *n1* is less than or equal to *n2*
n1 **-lt** *n2*   *n1* is smaller than *n2*
n1 **-ne** *n2*   *n1* is not equal to *n2*

Combinatoric conditions

! *a1*   true if expression *a1* is false
a1 **-a** *a2*   true if *a1* and *a2* are true
a1 **-o** *a2*   true if *a1* or *a2* is true

Examples

```
if [ -f /etc/shadow ]
```
       tests whether file /etc/shadow exists

if ["$res" != "j"]

> Does the content of the variable res equal "j"?

while [-z "$res"]

> Does the variable res contain an empty string?

---

time command [arguments]

time

Executes the specified command and then displays the execution time.

---

touch [options] files

touch

Changes the last access date/time and the last modification date/time of files. If a specified file does not exist, it is created as empty.

Available options

-a	changes only the time of the last access
-c	disables the creation of empty files for nonexistent ones
-m	changes only the time of the last modification
-r *file*	transfers the time from a specified reference *file*
-t *value*	sets the file date and the system time to the specified *value* with the format MMDDhhmm (month, day, hour, minute)

---

tr [options] [string1 [string2]]

tr

Copies the standard input device to the standard output device and in the process replaces or deletes characters. If a character from string1 is found in the standard input device, then it is replaced with the corresponding character from string2.

Available options

-c	outputs the complement of the set of characters in string1
-d	deletes characters that appear in string1
-s	suppresses repeated sequences in the output

troff [options] [files]

Formats files for printer or linotronic machine (also see nroff and groff)

---

true

This command returns only 0 ("successful") as return code. It is used primarily in shell scripts.

---

umask [value]

Outputs the current value of the file generation mask as an octal number or sets this value. This mask determines the maximum permissions that a newly created file can receive. Here the umask value is subtracted from the permissions of the file to be created.

---

uname [options]

Outputs the name and version number of the current system.

Available options

- **-a**   outputs all available information
- **-m**   outputs hardware (processor) type
- **-n**   outputs the host name
- **-r**   outputs the version number of the operating system
- **-s**   outputs the name of the operating system
- **-v**   outputs the date and time of compilation of the kernel

---

uncompress [options] [files]

Restores an original file that was compressed with compress .

Available options

- **-c**   outputs the file contents to the standard output device. Here uncompress behaves like the command zcat.

uniq [options] [file1 [file2]]

uniq

Deletes successive identical lines in the linewise sorted file1 and outputs these to file2 (or the standard output device).

Available options

-c	outputs the number of repetitions
-d	outputs only lines that occur redundantly
-u	outputs only lines that occur uniquely
-n	skips a number *n* of fields (with tabs and blanks as delimiters) before comparing two lines
+n	skips *n* characters before beginning to compare
-w	specifies the number of characters to be compared

uptime

uptime

Outputs the current time, the time since the last reboot, the number of logged users, and the momentary system load.

uudecode [file]

uudecode

Decodes a file encoded with uuencode using its original name, owner, and permissions

uuencode [file1] name

uuencode

Encodes binary files so that they can be represented as ASCII files and sent via e-mail. An encoded file is 35% larger than the original. The result is written to the standard output device. The specified name corresponds to the file name after the file is unpacked by its recipient.

vi [options] [files]

vi

Full-screen editor for processing ASCII files. It is largely based on ex and generally functions on all terminals.

w [options] [users]

Displays all currently logged users and their activities. Without parameters, all users are output; with a name, only the specified user.

Available options

-h   suppresses a title line
-f   determines whether the login terminal should also be output
-s   concise output format

---

wc [options] [files]

Counts the number of characters, words, and lines in a text file.

Available options

-c   only the number of characters
-l   only the number of lines
-w   only the number of words

---

whatis [commands]

Outputs a short description of the specified commands from the Online Manual

---

which [commands]

Outputs the file path of the specified commands (usually an internal shell command)

---

who [options] [file]

Outputs a list of currently users currently logged in, their terminals, the login time and the name of the host on which they logged in. If a file name is specified in addition, then this file is used for evaluation instead of /etc/utmp.

Available options

am i	outputs the user's own data
-i	outputs how long the user was inactive
-H	outputs column headings
-q	outputs only the login name and the number of users
-w	displays whether the user accepts (+) messages generated with `write` or not (-)

---

write `user [terminal]`

write

Outputs a message on a certain user's `terminal`. The message is read by the standard input device until it encounters EOF (**Ctrl** + **d**).

---

xargs `[options] [commands]`

xargs

Executes a `command` with the (multiple) arguments read from the standard input device. This enables passing lists of any length of arguments to commands.

Available options

-0	file names are terminated by the character null
-e *string*	ends processing as soon as the specified character *string* appears in the list of file names (default is "_")
-l *n*	executes the command with *n* arguments
-n *n*	executes the command with at most *n* arguments
-p	interactive processing where the user must respond with "y" before a command is executed
-s *n*	the whole command line may contain at most *n* characters
-t	displays the command before its execution

---

zcat `[files]`

zcat

Decompresses the specified `files` and outputs their contents to the standard output device. The compressed files remain untouched.

Index